Retire with
JIM HANNA

A COMPREHENSIVE GUIDE ADDRESSING
ALL YOUR RETIREMENT NEEDS

JIM HANNA

This document discusses general concepts for retirement planning, and is not intended to provide tax or legal advice. Individuals are urged to consult with their tax and legal professionals regarding these issues. This handbook should ensure that clients understand a) that annuities and some of their features have costs associated with them; b) that income received from annuities is taxable; and c) that annuities used to fund IRAs do not afford any additional measure of tax deferral for the IRA owner.

Printed in the United States of America

First Printing, 2014

Gradient Positioning Systems, LLC
4105 Lexington Avenue North, Suite 110
Arden Hills, MN 55126 (877) 901-0894

ACKNOWLEDGMENTS

First, I would like to thank my wife, Barbie, for her support and love. To my close personal friend and our attorney Bill Gremillion, who has been a tremendous asset to me, and our clients, thank you. Also, I would like to thank my assistant, Irma Lewis, her contributions for the past six years have been essential to the success of this company. Finally, I would like to thank Nick Stovall, Mike Binger, Nate Lucius and Gradient Positioning Systems, LLC for their contributions to this project.

TABLE OF CONTENTS

INTRODUCTION

Carol is a school teacher and the daughter of a World War II veteran. When her mother passed away this past year, she left Carol a $300,000 inheritance. At the age of 62, Carol and her husband, Dan, are still working. Dan is also a teacher doing part-time sub work and Carol works full-time because neither of them thinks they have saved enough for retirement. They are worried about outliving their money and affording health care once they both stop working and are no longer insured through their employer. They experienced first-hand the high costs of long term care when Dan's father had to be moved to an assisted living facility. Even though Dan and Carol are looking forward to their retirement years, several unknowns loom in front of them. How long should they keep working? When should they start Social Security? What is the best way to invest their inheritance money and would that money be enough? Carol has savings in her *teacher retirement plan and Dan has a small amount in his, but they don't know how to utilize that money, what it is currently invested in, or how to structure their assets so they won't incur a huge tax debt. With all these questions weighing down on them, they decide to seek guidance from the financial professional who had once helped Carol's mom.*

Many retirees today face so many challenges they are downright scared to go into retirement. They are working longer and harder because they don't know if they will have enough funds to keep up with the rising costs of health care, taxes and the unpredictability of the stock market. The majority of their fears have to do with stock market loss, outliving their money and health concerns that for many middle-class Americans can make retirement seem more like a nightmare than a dream.

NIGHTMARES ON RETIREMENT STREET

Investments and retirement savings represent one of the largest areas where there is a huge knowledge gap between what people have and what they think they have. Like Carol and Dan, they signed up for the program offered at work and for the past 20 or 30 years, they have been busy – raising their families, paying off debt and going to work. Saving the money was hard enough. Understanding how that money is invested is not something most people take the time to do. The stock market downturn of 2008 got a lot of people's attention.

Stock market loss is a fear foremost on the minds of most retirees. In the fall of 2008, many senior citizens went to bed at night and woke up the next morning with over 40 percent of their retirement savings gone. They had to delay retirement, sell their homes or start looking for employment because the really terrifying thing about losing money in the stock market is that once that money is gone, it's gone. There is no cure, no magic investment and no one to sue to get that money back. Today's retirees have the weight of that responsibility on their shoulders. What might the market bring in the future? It can get pretty scary for someone going into retirement today who is still in the market and doesn't quite understand the ramifications of what that means. That's why basic education about 401(k) plans, IRAs and stock market investments is one of the first things we focus on when building a plan for retirement.

Outliving your money is another fear haunting today's senior citizens. The medical community, doctors and scientists have put us in a position now where our life expectancy is getting longer and longer. Obviously this is a concern because the longer we live, the more it will cost us. How much longer are retirees living today? According to the Social Security administration, the average man in 1950 lived to be 65 years old and the average woman lived to be 71. Today, men are living an average of 19 years longer and women an average of 15 years longer, which means if you retire at age 65 today, you need to plan for at least 20 more years of income.*

Health concerns are hot on the heels of longevity concerns. As we get older, our bodies get tired and start to wear out. What happens if you need hip replacement surgery or costly medication? How will you afford the additional expense? According to a 2011 Fidelity Investments study, a 65-year-old couple would need an additional $230,000 of income to pay for medical expenses throughout their retirement years, and this figure doesn't even include long term care expenses. As a country, we don't really know where we are going with regard to insurance and health care issues. We are already seeing the government cutting back more and more on senior health care services, which makes this scenario

---

*http://www.ncbi.nlm.nih.gov/books/NBK62373/

even more grim. Many people are already facing this situation as they watch parents or loved one go through the aging process.

THE SANDWICH GENERATION

Living longer means we have more time to do the things we want to do with the people we love the most, but it comes with a cost. As a 62 year-old senior citizen getting ready to retire, Dan in our story above has a mother and father both still living and in their late 80s. Like 69 percent of people who live to be in their 90s, Dan's parents struggle with disability issues that have depleted their financial resources.* Dan and his sister divided up the work of caring for mom and dad, both of them sacrificing their jobs and going down to part-time status so they could help out. When Dan's father became bed-bound, the emotional and physical stress of it became too much. Dan and his sister moved their father into a full-time care facility. Dan and his sister also agreed to help mom and dad with the expense.

As if that weren't enough, the cost of college tuition is another responsibility draining the savings out of many retirees' bank accounts. Parents want to help their kids get through college with a minimum of debt, with graduate and post-graduate opportunities. If you have more than one child, this cost can really add up, especially when it's combined with the cost of helping out mom and dad. Hence the "sandwich" many retirees find themselves in the middle of, caught between both of these important care-giver "roles."

SOLVING THE PROBLEM OF RETIREMENT TODAY

With all of these concerns, it's no wonder so many of today's retirees are feeling overwhelmed. Retirement today is a self-directed and self-implemented enterprise. Growing your savings so they

---

*http://longtermcare.gov/the-basics/who-needs-care/

can keep up with inflation isn't as easy as it once used to be. The global economy and government debt-reduction buyouts have made the stock market an increasingly volatile and unsafe place to hold your retirement savings. The alternative – putting your money in safe vehicles such as bonds and certificates of deposit (CDs) – can't keep up with inflation. Solving the retirement dilemma today requires you to be knowledgeable and educated about the investment tools out there designed to solve the problems particular to retiring today.

During your working years, you work, you save, and you pay off debt. As your money grows in the investment vehicles you have chosen, there are no regular withdrawals, and any losses due to stock market corrections are mitigated by time and the steady influx of deposits coming from your paycheck. Once you enter into your pre-and-post retirement years, however, all that changes. When you stop working, there are no more steady paychecks, and no more deposits going into your savings account. What happens now is you start to take that money out. You make a switch out of the accumulation phase of life and into the payout phase. Preparing for this step begins with an examination of lifestyle, an assessment of income needs, and a restructuring of available assets.

USING THE RIGHT TOOLS AND ACQUIRING KNOWLEDGE

The purpose of this book is to help educate and inform you about the different tools, strategies and products available for retirees facing the income challenges of retiring today. These tools are designed to help solve the problems of stock market volatility, longevity concerns and unexpected expenses during the payout phase of life. We will also cover many subjects that have nothing to do with financial products but everything to do with knowledge and your peace of mind.

Lifestyle Considerations: Where do you want to live during retirement? How do you expect your lifestyle to change as you age? Where you live during your golden years often has a large impact on how you live. Lifestyle considerations such as health and family have a surprisingly large impact on the amount of finances you'll need to secure the future of your retirement income.

Asset Protection: Do you know what you are invested in? Do you lie awake at night worried that a downturn in the stock market could wipe out your retirement account? Understanding how much of your savings are at risk, and exactly how much risk they are exposed to, is a crucial step in a planful approach to retirement and the subject of our second chapter, *How Do You Feel About Losing Money?*

Social Security Maximization: Almost half of all senior citizens file for Social Security early at the age of 62, resulting in a 25 percent reduction in benefits.* There are a few good reasons to do this, but filing because you don't know any better is a bad reason. Once you begin taking your Social Security benefit for one year, that amount is locked in for the rest of your life. Taking this benefit at the wrong time and not understanding how to maximize what you receive using techniques such as file and suspend and spousal benefits can cost you thousands of dollars over the lifetime of your benefit.

Aid and Attendance: Aid and Attendance (A&A) is a little known benefit funded by Congress in 2001 for qualifying wartime veterans and their surviving spouses. The benefit is paid in addition to their monthly pension and increases yearly according to the Social Security cost of living increase. The benefit is designed to assist veterans or their spouses paying out of pocket for long term care and is available to individuals who reside in assisted

---

*When to Claim Social Security Benefits, David Blanchett, CFA, CFP° January, 2013

living communities, personal care homes, skilled nursing facilities and those receiving personal in-home care.*

New Investment Tools: New products such as today's Fixed Indexed Annuities (FIAs) and enhanced insurance products such as Indexed Universal Life (IULs) are available to all retirees. These products used alone or in a combined strategy known as laddering can solve several problems at once including provisions for lifetime income, long term care and tax efficiency.

Tax Strategies: Perhaps the most impactful piece of retirement planning is determining your current and future tax liability and developing strategies to minimize the amount of taxes you pay out during retirement. Tax planning can have a huge effect on the amount of wealth you will be able to transfer to your legacy. It also affects the bottom line of your annual income. Tax planning structures your assets to utilize both tax advantaged and taxable products, ensuring that you and your heirs are maximizing wealth for generations to come.

WHAT DOES RETIRING WITH JIM HANNA MEAN?

Jim Hanna has been licensed to serve in the financial industry since 1981. During those 33 years, he has seen it all: wars, taxes and national debt. People had their worries back then, but they also had a pension *plus* Social Security. People felt that the company they worked for was going to take care of them, or the government would take care of them. Today's reality is telling us something different. What most retirees are hearing today is that when it comes to retirement, *you are on your own.*

Retiring with Jim Hanna means you don't have to go it alone.

Retire with Jim Hanna is a full-service planning company serving San Antonio, Texas, and the surrounding communities, committed to helping you create a retirement plan that will help

*http://www.veteranaid.org/program.php

bring you both financial security and peace of mind. Our mission is to provide families and businesses with financial clarity, innovative strategies and solutions to not just help you retire, but to improve the quality of your life.

Founder and CEO Jim Hanna is a Veteran of the Viet Nam era and an experienced Veterans Accredited Claims Agent with a passion for assisting veterans and their spouses. Working in concert with licensed securities agents, estate planning attorneys and a partnership with local CPA firms, Retire With Jim Hanna can provide a comprehensive retirement plan that fits your needs today while providing for future needs in the years to come.

Many financial professionals focus on products; our experience shows us that your needs are best met by focusing on *you*. Making strong commitments to our clients and building life-long relationships are tenets of success at Retire With Jim Hanna because when you work with us, you have a partner for life.

1
LIFESTYLE CHOICES AND CHANGES

"Can we afford the same kind of lifestyle in retirement that we've grown accustomed to?"

Money represents more than the paper it's printed on. It is the embodiment of your time, your talents, and your commitments. It buys the food you eat, the house you sleep in, the car you drive, and the clothes you wear. It also helps provide you with the lifestyle you want to live once you retire.

The question on most retirees' minds is not can I retire, but can I retire and live the same lifestyle I am accustomed to? Taking this question even further is the consideration, can I afford to maintain this lifestyle for another 10, 20 or even 30 years down the road? The minute you quit working and the income stops, a bit of reality starts to set in as people realize what they can and can't do now that they are no longer working. That's the lifestyle shock. It's easy to think you won't spend as much money once you stop working, but most people find this isn't the case. There are statistics out there that suggest even after entering into retirement, your expenses are not going to change. The 80 percent rule states that you will still have 80 percent of your current expenses once entering into retirement. If that statistic is true for you, then you've got to be paying attention to cash flow.

How much of that cash flow you can control has a lot to do with lifestyle. There are also several life situations that come up during retirement that are completely out of your control. Having a discussion up front about these choices and changes ensures that your retirement plan fits both your short term and long term needs.

DISCOVERY OF LIFESTYLE

One of the most important things to be aware of as you approach your retirement is all the different things that change during this stage of your life and as a result influence lifestyle changes. Planning for retirement will ensure that those changes are for the better. Your retirement income – or how much money you have coming in every month – is of concern to everybody as they get closer to the day the paychecks stop coming. But before we set about designing an income plan that maximizes your assets and stretches every dollar, we need to look realistically at the changes that are coming around the corner. Obviously, the more income you have, the better you will able to adapt to those changes. Planning for those changes also ensures you have the right amount of money at the right time.

A discovery of your current and future lifestyle begins with a series of questions about family. Most of you won't be all that surprised to hear that family has a big effect on cash flow. We start the lifestyle discovery with a talk about the people closest to you, about their needs and your responsibilities. This process includes questions such as:

- Do you have special needs children?
- Where do your parents live and how old are they?
- Are you married? Divorced? On a second or third marriage?
- Do you have any siblings?

If these questions sound like they are personal, it's because they are. A good retirement plan is personal because every number is attached to the people and circumstances of your life. Most people are surprised to find themselves talking about their recreational activities, hobbies and how many times they go on vacation, where go and what they do.

- What is your social life like?
- Do you play golf? Run, bike, do yoga or swim?
- What activities are you involved in?

The social aspect of your lifestyle gives you a great many clues as to what kind of discretionary income will likely be needed in the years to come. The answers to these questions also give a peek into your health. In many ways, talking with a financial professional about your retirement plans is like seeking the help of a medical doctor. Your health is probably one of the most critical pieces to uncover during the first meeting. It can be a delicate subject, but your health and medical issues impact many important decisions such as:

- When are you hoping to retire?
- What are your goals during retirement?
- What do you picture yourself doing during your retirement years?

As we get further into our discussion, we'll also talk about your retirement timeline, needs, wants, values and goals. When deciding on whether or not an investment is a good fit for you, the answers to these questions are the core considerations that can help a professional determine which investment tools are best for you.

YOUR RETIREMENT TIMELINE

Getting to the bottom of things, in order to know when you want to retire, it's good to understand why you want to retire. There are three reasons (besides money) that people usually have for wanting to retire soon. Those reasons are: job dissatisfaction, health concerns and family issues. It's important for your financial professional to understand your reasons because knowing this affects the kind of investments tools and products they will recommend on your behalf.

- Job dissatisfaction: If you are unhappy at your current job, making the decision to delay retirement by two or three years so you can roll up your Social Security benefit might not be an option for you. Job dissatisfaction combined with health concerns means it's imperative you consider the trade-off involved when trying to get a higher lifetime benefit. If you aren't enjoying your life, then what's it all for?
- Health concerns: This reason alone comes with many powerful lifestyle considerations. It affects where you live, whether or not you sell the house and move to an apartment, whether or not you want a living space with stairs, how far you are away from family and whether or not you have provisions for long term care needs.
- Family issues: It is amazing the lengths that people will go to for the people that they love. If your daughter is going through a divorce and she needs to borrow money to buy

a house in a safe neighborhood for the grandkids, and you have the money sitting in an IRA, can you say no? Most people find that they cannot. Helping mom and dad pay for their long term care is another issue that often comes up. There are financial tools out there designed to grow your money future needs such as these if they are planned for at the outset.

Waiting until disaster strikes is usually too late to plan for contingencies such as family emergencies or a health crisis. Having the conversation now about these life issues means you'll have the money down the road to do what is best for you and your family.

FACT OF LIFE DISCUSSIONS

The one true thing about life is that it is filled with change. Our bodies are no exception. As we grow older and live longer into retirement, our bodies start to slow down and go through their own set of changes. Health issues come up and we end up spending more time in the doctor's office. Our outlook on maintaining good health becomes more of a priority and we start to become more conscious about what we eat and how much we exercise we get. If we do these things diligently, we hope to stay a little ahead of the aging game, but sooner or later, we find ourselves on the wagon and part of the health care system. Questions have to be dealt with such as where will I live? How will I get around? And who will help take care of me?

One thing that often comes up during these discussions is the house. What is your current living situation? Is the house paid off? Do you have a second mortgage? A home equity loan? As houses get older they are also subject to the wear and tear of time. In addition to regular maintenance, they begin to need more and more repairs. How are you going to keep up with that? Sometimes our homes can become a deep hole we keep throwing money into as this breaks down and that breaks down. When your paychecks stop and you are living on a fixed income, you have to ask yourself, can I afford to keep doing this?

Taxes go up. Utilities go up. Cost of insurance goes up. But when we go into retirement and are on a fixed income, that doesn't go up.

Is it worth going deeper into debt to maintain the family home? Is this an emotional attachment that might be getting in the way of a good financial decision? Would you be better off living somewhere else? Some place without stairs? And if you are going to move, would it be better to move now rather than later, when a move will only be harder?

This is just one example of the kinds of fact of life discussions that end up bearing financial importance. Lifestyle changes are coming down the road. Those changes will impact our how and where we live, and that in turn will have an effect on our finances. Discussing health care and housing needs now and coming up with a plan means you will be able to financially adapt to these change and approach your final years with grace and dignity.

THE IMPORTANCE OF A PLANFUL APPROACH

The way you approach your retirement impacts your income, the taxes your assets are subject to, your financial stability in the future, and your legacy. It is a truism among financial professionals that one hour of organizing your assets can be worth more than an entire lifetime of working and saving when it comes to retirement. Why is this so?

The fact of the matter is that after working and saving for a lifetime, entering retirement changes all of the rules you have known and followed for your entire career. Instead of an earning and saving paradigm, you are moving into an income and asset leveraging paradigm where you need to use the money you have earned and saved to generate income and preserve your assets for you. Making sure your assets last for your lifetime will depend on how you decide to invest them, and in what order you will spend them

Advice about what to do with money has been around as long as money has existed. Hindsight allows us to see which advice was good and which advice didn't cut the mustard. Some sources of advice have been around for a very long time. While there are some basic investment concepts that have stood the test of time, most strategies that work adapt to changing conditions in the market, in the economy and the world, as well as changes in your personal circumstances.

The reality is that investment strategies and savings plans that worked in the past have encountered challenging new circumstances that have turned them on their heads. The Great Recession of the early 2000's highlighted how old investment ideas were not only ineffective but incredibly destructive to the retirement plans of millions of Americans. The dawn of an entirely restructured health care system brings with it new options and challenges that will undoubtedly change the way insurance companies provide investment products and services.

Perhaps the most important lessons investors learned from the Great Recession is that not understanding where your money is invested (and the potential risks of those investments) can work against you, your plans for retirement and your legacy. Saving and investing money isn't enough to truly get the most out of it. You must have a planful approach to managing your assets.

Essentially, managing your money and your investments is an ongoing process that requires customization and adaptation to a changing world. And make no mistake; the world is always changing. What worked for your parents or even your parents' parents was probably good advice back then. People in retirement or approaching retirement today need new ideas and professional guidance.

CHAPTER 1 RECAP //

- How much cash flow you will need during your retirement years has a lot to do with lifestyle. There are lifestyle choices you can change such as where you live and what social activities you participate in. There are also many lifestyle changes coming down the road that you can't change. Having a discussion up front about these choices and changes ensures that your retirement plan fits both your short term and long term needs.

- The reasons why you want to retire are as important as when you want to retire. The three main reasons people have for wanting to retire are job dissatisfaction, health concerns and family issues. These considerations must be mentioned up front so your financial professional can recommend investment tools that are right for your situation.

- It is a fact of life that as we get older, our bodies change. As these changes take place, our daily needs and housing considerations may need to adapt. Having a discussion about the realities of these changes up front means the changes can be planned for so you can live your retirement years with greater dignity.

- The rules for retirement planning have changed. Investing the way your parents did will not pay off and the majority of investment ideas used by financial professionals in the 1990s aren't applicable to today's markets. That kind of investing will likely get you in trouble and compromise your retirement. Today, you need a better PLAN. Having a planful approach to retirement gives consideration to today's stock market and economy, and the individual concerns of you, the investor.

2

HOW DO YOU FEEL ABOUT LOSING MONEY?

"Do you have the right investments?"

Maggie is 65 years old and wants to retire in two years. She has a 401(k) from her job to which she has contributed for 26 years. She also has some stocks that her late husband managed. Maggie also has $55,000 in a mutual fund that her sister recommended to her five years ago and $30,000 in another mutual fund that she heard about at work. She takes a look at her assets one day and decides that she doesn't understand what they add up to or what kind of retirement they will provide. She decides to meet with an investment professional. During their second meeting Maggie's professional asks her:

1. **Does she know exactly where all of her money is?** *Maggie doesn't know much about all her husband's stocks, which have now become hers. Their value is at $100,000 invested in three large cap companies. Maggie is unsure of the companies and whether she should hold or sell them.*

2. **Does she know what types of assets she owns?** *Yes and no. She knows she had a 401(k) and IRAs, but she is unfamiliar with her husband's self-directed stock portfolio or the type of mutual funds she owns. Furthermore she is unclear as to how to manage the holdings as she nears retirement.*

3. **Does she know the strategies behind each one of the investment products she owns?** *While Maggie knows she had a 401(k), an IRA and mutual fund holdings, she doesn't know how her 401(k) is organized or how to make it more conservative as she nears retirement. She is unsure whether her IRA is a Roth or traditional variety and how to draw income from them? She really does not have specific investment principles guiding her investment decisions, and she doesn't know anything about her husband's individual stocks. One major concern for Maggie is whether her family would be okay if she were not around?*

After determining Maggie's assets, her financial professional prepares a consolidated report that lays out all of her assets for her to review. Her professional explains each one of them to her. Maggie discovers that although she is two years away from retiring, her 401(k) is organized with an amount of risk with which she is not comfortable. Sixty percent of her 401(k) is at risk and would suffer a reduction in value were the stock market to take a downturn. Maggie will rely on her 401(k) for most of her immediate income needs after retirement and did not realize the future of her retirement income was sitting at risk.

Maggie's professional also points out several instances of overlap between her mutual funds. Maggie learns that while she is comfortable with one of her mutual funds, she does not agree with the manage-

ment principles of the other. In the end, Maggie's professional helps her re-organize her 401(k) to secure her nest egg for retirement income. Her professional also uses her mutual fund and her husband's stock assets to create a growth oriented investment plan that Maggie will rely on 15 years down the road when she plans on relocating closer to her children and grandchildren. By creating an overall investment strategy that takes into consideration risk factors and lifestyle changes, Maggie is able to meet her targeted goals in retirement. Maggie's financial professional also worked closely with her tax professional to minimize the tax impact of any asset sales on Maggie's situation as they re-structured her investments.

Like Maggie, you may have several savings vehicles: a 401(k), an IRA to which you regularly contribute, some mutual funds to which you make monthly contributions, etc. But what is your *overall investment strategy*? Do you have one in place? Do you want one that will help you meet your retirement goals?

You spend your entire working life hoping what you put into your retirement accounts will help you live comfortably once you clock out of the workforce for good. The key word in that sentiment and the word that can make retirement feel like a looming problem instead of a rewarding life stage, is hope. Like Maggie, you *hope* you'll have enough money. Many people like Maggie rely on their company 401(k) plan as their primary vehicle for savings, but most people don't pay much attention to what those investments are doing. Some people find they have multiple accounts if they left a job but kept their money in the company plan. These investments could be all over the spectrum as far risk goes, yet most people have no idea as to the amount of risk their savings are exposed to.

You've got to find out as soon as you can what investments you have and what kind of risk those assets are exposed to. It's vital to the safety of your retirement nest egg that you have a comprehensive strategy when it comes to risk. Approaching retirement means you should be moving toward a more conservative approach. Structuring those assets in safe money vehicles that can still keep up with inflation and generate the income you need requires a financial strategy for the pay-out phase of your retirement years. Add to this the complexities of taxes, required minimum distributions (RMDs) from IRAs and legacy planning, and you can begin to see why happy endings require more than hope. They need a focused and well-executed plan.

Understanding how to manage your assets entails risk management, risk diversification, tax planning and income planning preparation throughout your life stages. These strategies can help you leverage more from each one of the hard-earned dollars you set aside for your retirement.

HOPE SO VS. KNOW SO MONEY

Let's take a look at some of the basic truths about money as it relates to saving for retirement.

There are essentially two kinds of money: *Hope So* and *Know So*. Everyone can divide their money into these two categories. Some have more of one kind than the other. The goal isn't to eliminate one kind of money but to balance them as you approach retirement.

Hope So Money is money that is at risk. It fluctuates with the market. It has no minimum guarantee. It is subject to investor activity, stock prices, market trends, buying trends, etc. You get the picture. This money is exposed to more risk but also has the potential for more reward. Because the market is subject to change, you can't really be sure what the value of your investments will be worth in the future. You can't really *rely* on it at all. For this reason, we refer to it as Hope So Money. This doesn't mean you shouldn't have some money invested in the market, but it would be dangerous to assume you can know what it will be worth in the future.

Hope So Money is an important element of a retirement plan, especially in the early stages of planning when you can trade volatility for potential returns, and when a longer investment timeframe is available to you. In the long run, time can smooth out the ups and downs of money exposed to the market. Working with a professional and leveraging a long-term investment strategy has the potential to create rewarding returns from Hope So Money.

Know So Money, on the other hand, is safer when compared to Hope So Money. Know So Money is made up of dependable,

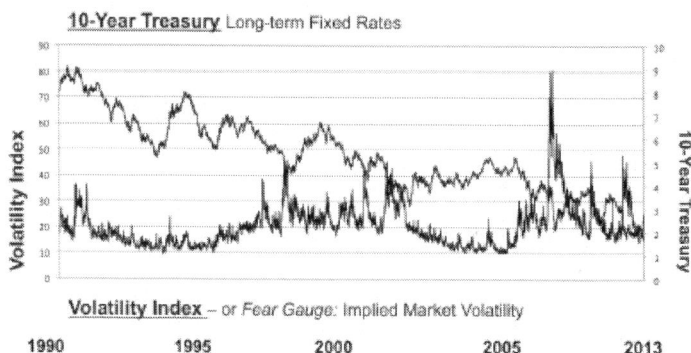

The VIX, or volatility index, of the market represents expected market volatility. When the VIX drops, economic experts expect less volatility. When the VIX rises, more volatility is expected.

1. *VIX is a trademarked ticker symbol for the Chicago Board Options Exchange (CBOE) Market Volatility Index, a popular measure of the implied volatility of S&P 500 index options. Often referred to as the fear index or the fear gauge, it represents one measure of the market's expectation of stock market volatility over the next 30 day period. (wikipedia.com)*

2. *The CBOE 10-Year Treasury Note (TNX) is based on 10 times the yield-to-maturity on the most recently auctioned 10-year Treasury note.*

low-risk or no-risk money, and investments that you can count on. Social Security is one of the most common forms of Know So Money. Income you draw or will draw from Social Security is guaranteed. You have paid into Social Security your entire career, and you can rely on that money during your retirement. Unlike the market, rates of growth for Know So Money are dependent on 10-year treasury rates. The 10-year treasury, or TNX, is commonly considered to represent a very secure and safe place for your money, hence Know So Money. The 10-year treasury drives key rates for things such as mortgage rates or CD rates. Know So Money may not be as exciting as Hope So Money, but it is safer. You can safely be fairly sure you will have it in the future.

Knowing the difference between Hope So and Know So Money is an important step towards a successful retirement plan. People who are 55 or older and who are looking ahead to retirement should be relying on more Know So Money than Hope So Money.

UNDERSTANDING THE RISK COMPONENT OF YOUR INVESTMENTS

Many investors don't know how much risk they are exposed to. It is helpful to organize your assets so you can have a clear understanding of how much of your money is at risk and how much is in safer holdings. This process starts with listing all your assets.

Let's take a look at the two kinds of money:

Hope So Money is, as the name indicates, money that you *hope* will be there when you need it. Hope So Money represents what you would like to get out of your investments. Examples of Hope So Money include:

- Stock market funds, including index funds
- Mutual funds
- Variable annuities

- REITS

Know So Money is money that you know you can count on. It is safer money that isn't exposed to the level of volatility as the asset types noted above. You can more confidently count on having this money when you need it. Examples of Know So Money are:
- Government backed bonds
- Savings and checking accounts
- Fixed income annuities
- CDs
- Treasuries
- Money market accounts

There is also a certain amount of risk inherent in investments that you don't understand, regardless of how those investments are designed to function. Not being knowledgeable about risk, distribution and tax liabilities of your investments can cost you thousands of dollars down the road if you are not aware of certain repercussions. Let's take a look at some of the common mistakes retirees make due to lack of knowledge:

Risk: An investment isn't good or bad because of the risk it is exposed to; it's good or bad according to *your retirement timeline.* The difference between risk during your working years versus your retirement years can be boiled down to one word: time. When you are young, you have more time to absorb risk. As you get older and your retirement years get closer, you don't have the six to eight years it takes to recover from a stock market loss because you need that money to pay the bills. If you have saved up money in a 401(k), for example, and that money is placed in aggressive, growth-focused mutual funds, you should be aware that you run the risk of losing a chunk of your retirement savings if a market downturn occurs. If you need that money to retire on in one to three years, you won't have enough time to grow that money back because once it's gone, it's gone. You need to know that there is a more conservative approach you can take, and that the ideal time to take that approach is during the five to ten years before you enter into retirement.

Distribution: Not understanding the rules associated with the distribution of your Individual Retirement Accounts (IRAs) can cost you thousands of dollars in penalties and taxes. With a traditional IRA account, your annual Required Minimum Distributions, or RMDs, begin to take place in the year you turn 70 ½. This is a birthday that's easy to miss, but the federal government will be paying attention. If you don't set up your RMDs in a timely manner, you could be subject to a 50 percent penalty. Combine that with the taxes you could owe after being put in a different income tax bracket, and this mistake can end up costing you thousands of retirement dollars.

Tax liabilities: Many people don't understand that the money they have been tucking away in their traditional IRA or 401(k) account is a tax liability. If you plan on leaving this money to your children, you have basically created a tax bomb. Why? Because this money was taken out of your paycheck **before** the taxes were paid. Those taxes have to be paid eventually, either by you or your beneficiaries. The questions is, over how many years will those tax payments be spread out? The consequences of not structuring your assets can result in a weighty tax liability for yourself and your heirs. Here's why:

Let's say you have been tucking away $5,500 a year. This was money that was automatically deducted from your paycheck so you never even saw it. The money was funneled directly to an IRA or 401(k) account and this was a good deal because at the end of the year, you were not taxed on this income. However, over the years, that money grows and really starts to add up; and the tax man is standing by, waiting to get his share of the money.

The absolute latest you can start paying the tax man his share is April 15 of the year following that magic date you reach 70 ½. At that point, taxes come due. The amount you owe in taxes is calculated by the Federal government based on average lifetime expectancy rates. So if you owe, for example, $70,000 in taxes, that amount will be divided by the number of years they calculate that you have left to live. Should you leave this earth and pass that money on to your beneficiaries, you also pass onto them your tax debt. Not only do they have to pay the taxes on the money that you earned, but they have to pay it according to the federal guidelines of *your* life expectancy, and not theirs. This means they could have thousands of dollars due by the end of the year, payable to the IRS. Ouch.

It is possible to avoid this. There is more than one way to avoid the big tax bomb. You can re-allocate the money into an annuity, or convert to a Roth IRA. You can also set the IRA up with a designated beneficiary. This gives your loved ones the ability to inherit the IRA as what's known as a Stretch IRA. With a Stretch IRA, the tax liability is spread out over the course of *their* lifetime, which significantly reduces the amount of the tax burden they owe at the end of each year.

> » *Wade had a modest brokerage account that he added to when he could. When he changed jobs a couple years ago, at age 58, Wade transferred his 401(k) assets into an IRA. Just a few years from retirement, he is now beginning to realize that nearly every dollar he has saved for retirement is subject to market risk.*
>
> *Intuitively, he knows that the time has come to shift some assets to an alternative that is safer, but how much is the right amount? What should he consider as far distribution, tax liabilities and risk? How can he organize his investments so*

they are structured with enough risk for growth and enough safety to allow for the protection of his income?

THE COLORS OF YOUR INVESTMENTS

To explain the risk inherent in your investments, it can be helpful to organize your assets into a visual schematic. We use the colors red, green and yellow to identify the different levels of risk your money is exposed to according the investment type. For our purposes, Know So Money (which is safer and more dependable) is green. Hope So Money (which is exposed to risk and fluctuates with the market) is red. Yellow money is Red Money that is being professionally managed. It has risk associated with it, but because this money is under the watchful eye of a professional, that risk is mitigated. The professional managing your money should know not just about the investments, but about you – what you need the money for and how you expect the investment to perform. A financial professional can help you better understand the colors of the money in your investment portfolio.

The fact of the matter is that a lot of people don't know their level of exposure to risk. Visually organizing your assets is an important and powerful way to get a clear picture of what kind of money you have, where it is and how you can best use it in the future. This process is as simple as listing your assets and assigning

Green Money	Red Money
"Green Money" is safer.	"Red Money" is at risk.
This is money that offers a minimum guarantee but it may pose risks other than market risk.	This is money that can go up or down in value. It may pose risk if it is not properly managed to serve a specific purpose in a comprehensive plan.

them a color based on their status as Hope So or Know So Money. Work with your financial professional to create a comprehensive inventory of your assets to understand what you are working with before making any decisions. This may be the first time you have ever sat down and sorted out all of your assets, allowing you to see how much money you have at risk in the market. Comparing the color of your investments will give you an idea of how near or far you are from adhering to the Rule of 100.

THE RULE OF 100: HOW MUCH RISK ARE YOU COMFORTABLE WITH?

Determining the amount of risk that is right for you is dependent on a number of variables. You need to feel comfortable with where and how you are investing your money, and your financial professional is obligated to help you make decisions that put your money in places that fit your risk criteria.

Your retirement needs to first accommodate your day-to-day income needs. How much money do you need to maintain your lifestyle? When do you need it?

Managing your risk by having a balance of Hope So Money vs. Know So Money is a good start that will put you ahead of the curve. But how much Know So Money is enough to secure your income needs during retirement, and how much Hope So Money is enough to allow you to continue to benefit from an improving market?

In short, how do you begin to know how much risk you should be exposed to?

While there is no single approach to investment risk determination advice that is universally applicable to everyone, there are some helpful guidelines. One of the most useful is called *The Rule of 100*.

The average investor needs to accumulate assets to create a retirement plan that provides income during retirement and also allows for legacy planning. To accomplish this, they need to balance the amount of risk to which they are exposed. Risk is required because, while Safe Side Money is safer, more reliable and more dependable, it doesn't grow very fast, if at all. Today's historically low interest rates barely break even with current inflation. Risk Side Money, while less dependable, has more potential for growth. Risk Side Money can eventually become Safe Side Money once you move it to an investment with lower risk. Everyone's risk diversification will be different depending on their goals, age and their existing assets.

So how do you decide how much risk *your* assets should be exposed to? Where do you begin? Luckily, there's a guideline you can use to start making decisions about risk management. It's called the Rule of 100.

CALCULATING YOUR RISK NUMBER

The Rule of 100 is a general rule that helps shape asset diversification* for the average investor. The rule states that the number 100 minus an investor's age equals the amount of assets they should have exposed to risk.

The Rule of 100: 100 - (your age) = the percentage of your assets that should be exposed to risk (Risk Side Money)

For example, if you are a 30-year-old investor, the Rule of 100 would indicate that you should be focusing on investing primarily in the market and taking on a substantial amount of risk in your

---

*Asset Diversification disclosure – Diversification and asset allocation does not assure of guarantee better performance and cannot eliminate the risk of investment loss. Before investing, you should carefully read the applicable volatility disclosure for each of the underlying funds, which can be found in the current prospectus.

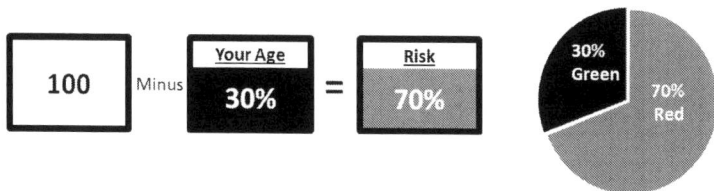

portfolio. The Rule of 100 suggests that 70 percent of your investments should be exposed to risk.

$$100 - (30 \text{ years of age}) = 70 \text{ percent}$$

Now, not every 30-year-old should have exactly 70 percent of their assets in mutual funds and stocks. The Rule of 100 is based on your chronological age, not your "financial age," which could vary based on your investment experience, your aversion or acceptance of risk and other factors. While this rule isn't an ironclad solution to anyone's finances, it's a pretty good place to start. Once you've taken the time to look at your assets with a professional to determine your risk exposure, you can use the Rule of 100 to make changes that put you in a more stable investment position — one that reflects your comfort level.

Perhaps when you were age 30 and starting your career, like in the example above, it made sense to have 70 percent of your money in the market: you had time on your side. You had plenty of time to save more money, work more and recover from a downturn in the market. Retirement was ages away, and your earning power was increasing. And indeed, younger investors should take on more risk for exactly those reasons. The potential reward of long-term involvement in the market outweighs the risk of investing when you are young.

Risk tolerance generally reduces as you get older, however. If you are 40 years old and lose 30 percent of your portfolio in a market downturn this year, you have 20 or 30 years to recover it. If you are 68 years old, you have five to ten years (or less) to make the same recovery. That new circumstance changes your whole retirement perspective. At age 68, it's likely that you simply aren't as interested in suffering through a tough stock market. There is less time to recover from downturns, and the stakes are higher. The money you have saved is money you will soon need to provide you with income, or is money that you already need to meet your income demands.

Much of the flexibility that comes with investing earlier in life is related to *compounding*. Compounded earnings can be incredibly powerful over time. The longer your money has time to compound, the greater your wealth will be. This is what most people talk about when they refer to putting their money to work. This is also why the Rule of 100 favors risk for the young. If you start investing when you are young, you can invest smaller amounts of money in a more aggressive fashion because you have the potential to make a profit in a rising market and you can harness the power of compounding earnings. When you are 40, 50 or 60 years old, that potential becomes less and less and you are forced to have more money at lower amounts of risk to realize the same returns. It basically becomes more expensive to prudently invest the older you get.

You risk not having a recovery period the older you get, so should have less of your assets at risk in volatile investments. You should shift with the Rule of 100 to protect your assets and ensure that they will provide you with the income you need in retirement. Let's look at another example that illustrates how the Rule of 100 becomes more critical as you age. An 80-year-old investor who is retired and is relying on retirement assets for income, for example, needs to depend on a solid amount of Safe Side Money. The Rule of 100 says an 80-year-old investor should have a maximum of

20 percent of his or her assets at risk. Depending on the investor's financial position, even less risk exposure may be required. You are the only person who can make this kind of determination, but the Rule of 100 can help. Everyone has their own level of comfort. Your Rule of 100 results will be based on your values and attitudes as well as your comfort with risk.

The Rule of 100 can apply to overarching financial management and to specific investment products that you own as well. Take the 401(k) for example. Many people have them, but not many people understand how their money is allocated within their 401(k). An employer may have someone who comes in once a year and explains the models and options that employees can choose from, but that's as much guidance as most 401(k) holders get. Many 401(k) options include target date funds that change their risk exposure over time, essentially following a form of the Rule of 100. Selecting one of these options can often be a good move for employees because they shift your risk as you age, securing more Safe Side Money when you need it.

A financial professional can look at your assets with you and discuss alternatives to optimize your balance between Safe Side and Risk Side Money.

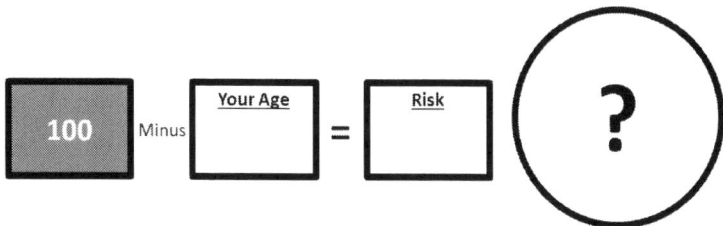

| 100 | Minus | Your Age | = | Risk | ? |

OPTIMIZING RISK AND FINDING THE RIGHT BALANCE

Determining the amount of risk that is right for you depends on your specific situation and lifestyle considerations. It starts by examining your particular financial position.

The Rule of 100 is a useful way to begin to deliberate the right amount of risk for you. But remember, it's just a baseline. Use it as a starting point for figuring out where your money should be. If you're a 50-year-old investor, the Rule of 100 suggests that you have 50 percent Safe Side Money and 50 percent Risk Side Money. Most 50-year-olds are more risk tolerant, however. There are many reasons why someone might be more risk tolerant, not the least of which is feeling young! Experienced investors, people who feel they need to gamble for a higher return, or people who have met their retirement income goals and are looking for additional ways to accumulate wealth are all candidates for investment strategies that incorporate higher levels of risk. In the end, it comes down to your personal tolerance for risk. How much are you willing to lose?

Consulting with a financial professional is often the wisest approach to calculating your risk level. A professional can help determine your risk tolerance by getting to know you, asking you a set of questions and even giving you a survey to determine your comfort level with different types of risk. Here's a typical scenario a financial professional might pose to you:

> *"You have $100,000 saved that you would like to invest in the market. There is an investment product that could turn your $100,000 into $120,000. That same option, however, has the potential of losing you up to $30,000, leaving you with $70,000."*

Is that a scenario that you are willing to enter into? Or are you more comfortable with this one:

"You could turn your $100,000 into $110,000, but have the potential of losing $15,000, leaving you with $85,000."

Your answer to these and others types of questions will help a financial professional determine what level of risk is right for you. They can then offer you investment strategies and management plans that reflect your financial age.

WORKING WITH A FINANCIAL PROFESSIONAL

Looking at lifestyle choices, discovering the risk value of your assets, and understanding the color of your money can quickly become an overwhelming task. The fact of the matter is that financial professionals build careers around understanding the different variables affecting retirement financing.

Working with a Registered Investment Advisor means working with a professional who is legally obligated to help you make financial decisions that are in your best interest and fall within your comfort zone. Taking steps toward creating a retirement plan is nothing to take lightly. By leveraging tax strategies, properly organizing your assets, and accumulating helpful financial products that help you meet your income and accumulation needs, you are more likely to meet your goals. You might have a million dollars socked away in a savings account, but your neighbor, who has $300,000 in a diverse investment portfolio that is tailored to their needs, may end up enjoying a better retirement lifestyle. Why? They had more than a good work ethic and a penchant for saving. They had a planful approach to retirement asset allocation.

CHAPTER 2 RECAP //

- Multiple retirement accounts can create confusion about risk, distribution requirements and tax liabilities. Taking control of your assets begins with determining your exposure to risk. Taking control of your assets also means answering the questions: *Do you know where your money is? Do you know what type of assets you own? Do you know the strategies behind your investment products?*

- Lack of knowledge can cost you retirement dollars in more ways than one. Educate yourself about the risk, distribution penalties and tax liabilities of all the investments you own.

- Understanding where and how your assets are invested is key to the safety of your retirement nest egg. With the help of a financial professional, it's easy to see what percentages of your assets are invested in risk, Hope So Money and safe, Know So Money.

- Assigning colors to money can help you more easily visualize the assets that make up your retirement savings. Green Money is safer and more reliable, Red Money represents assets that are exposed to risk, and Yellow Money is Red Money managed by a professional.

- Use the Rule of 100 as a general guiding principle when determining how much risk your retirement investments should be exposed to (100 - [your age] = [percentage of your investments that can comfortably be exposed to risk])

- Your exposure to risk is ultimately determined by you.

- Working with a Registered Investment Advisor will help you compose a clear and concise inventory of your assets, and learn how much they are worth, what rules apply to them, and how they are structured for risk. A Registered Investment Advisor is legally obligated to help you make financial decisions that are in your best interest and fall within your comfort zone. They can also help you structure your investments so as to reflect your goals, needs and objectives.

3

ARRIVING AT THE NUMBERS:
How Much Money Do You Need?

"Will we run out of money during retirement?"

An important aspect of your financial plan is the evaluation of your income needs. Finding the most efficient and beneficial way to address them will have impacts on your lifestyle, your asset accumulation and your legacy planning after you retire. Take a moment to think about your income goals:

- What is your lifestyle today?
- Would you like to maintain it into retirement?
- Are you meeting your needs?

- Are you happy with your lifestyle?
- What do you really *need* to live on when you retire?

Some people will have the luxury of maintaining or improving their lifestyle, while others may have to make decisions about what they need versus what they want during their retirement. Once you have identified your income need, you will know how much to structure for income now and how much to be set aside for accumulation and income needs down the road.

WHAT'S REALISTIC?

The easiest way to find out if you are on track when it comes to your income needs is to answer the simple question: in a perfect world, if you wanted to retire tomorrow, what would be the magic number that you need to hit your bank account every month? What would that figure be? Most people have a number in mind and that number will tell you a lot about your lifestyle.

Every financial strategy for retirement needs first to accommodate the day-to-day need for income. To answer the question—how much money do I need?—start with a household budget. Make a list of your expenses and divide them into two categories: **Expenses You Can't Control** and the **Expenses You Can Control**. Understand the difference between the two has a way of shedding light on any lifestyle changes that that might need to take place as you transition into retirement.

The moment your working income ceases and you start living off the money you've set aside for retirement is referred to as the retirement cliff. When you begin drawing income from your retirement assets, you have entered the distribution phase of your financial plan. **The distribution phase of your retirement plan** is when you reach the point of relying on your assets for income. This is where your Green Money comes into play: the safer, more reliable assets that you have accumulated that are designed to provide you with a steady income. On day one of your retirement, you will need a steady and reliable supply of income from your Green Money.

How Much Money Do You Need? While this amount will be different for everyone, the general rule of thumb is that a retiree will require 70 to 80 percent of their pre-retirement income to maintain their lifestyle. Once you know what that number is, the key becomes matching your income need with the correct investment strategies, options and tools to satisfy that need.

PLANNING FOR THE CONTINGENCIES

In addition to the day-to-day expenses of bills, food and discretionary spending, there is a third expense category many people don't plan for. This category is what we call "planning for the contingencies" and it includes health care expenses and long term care expenses for yourself and your spouse. **Statistics reveal that 70 percent of retirees age 65 today will need some form of long term care, and 20 percent of those cases will require care for five years or longer.*** If these expenses are planned for ahead of time, during the income-planning phase of retirement, you have a lot more options when it comes to paying for these expenses. If you are a veteran who is currently retired and already facing the financial demands of critical care costs, the Aid and Attendance benefit might be one solution available to you.

SOLUTIONS FOR FUNDING LONG TERM CARE:

- Group Funded Long Term Care: Your current employer might have a group-funded long term care package available. These are often available to teacher retirement pensions and government employees— before they retire. The election to maximize the benefits provided by your

---

*http://longtermcare.gov/the-basics/how-much-care-will-you-need/

pension must be done before you retire and is usually handled through your company Human Resource (HR) department. A month before you retire or up to three months after, you often have the option to make final decisions regarding these benefits.

- **Traditional Long Term Care Insurance:** This option allows you to transfer the risk of long term care to an insurance company. It works very similarly to house insurance, car insurance, and health insurance, where you pay out an annual premium. The longer you wait to purchase this type of insurance, the higher the risk that you won't qualify because it is your health that qualifies you for this type of insurance. Also, be aware that as you get older, the higher the cost of this type of insurance. The money you pay into this kind of policy can only be used to fund long term care costs as specified in the contract. If you end up not needing this type of care, the money you have paid into the policy reverts back to the insurance company.

- **Life Insurance Products:** Many of today's life insurance policies and annuity products have riders and provisions for increased income in the event of chronic illness. Often known as Living Benefits, these products provide you with the means to pay for home health care or a nursing home facility while you are still alive. With annuities, these benefits are known as "income doublers" because the fixed income contracted by the rider will double should you or your spouse require long term care. Long term care can include basic custodial services such as cleaning and taking out the garbage, or it can be more involved and include intrinsic nursing services. Even if it's too late to qualify for traditional long term care insurance, long term care riders on annuity and life insurance products might still be an option for you. Another benefit of this option is that these policies also have a death benefit, so even if you never need long term care, that money is not lost. Instead, your beneficiaries receive a legacy.

- **Self-Insure:** With this option, you take a portion of your assets, put it into a bucket marked for long term care, and invest in a safe Green Money type of investment. You and your spouse have to know that you won't need these funds for retirement income. Then if either you or your spouse needs to go into a facility, you know what funds to tap into.

- **Aid and Attendance:** This is one solution available to veterans and surviving spouses who require the regular attendance of another person to assist in bathing, dressing, feeding (not to include meal preparation), mobility (assistance with getting in or out of a chair or bed), hygiene (brushing teeth or toileting), or supervision due to cognitive impairment. The veteran or spouse must be paying out of pocket for this assistance (or self-insuring.) This benefit is available to individuals who reside in assisted living communities, personal care homes, skilled nursing facilities and those receiving personal in-home care. Military eligibility is the first requirement.

  - The veteran must have served in active military for 90 or more consecutive days, with one day during a period of wartime as defined by the Veterans Administration.

  - The veteran must have been discharged under anything other than dishonorable conditions.

  - The veteran must be at least 65 years of age or totally and permanently disabled.

  - A surviving spouse of a war veteran may be eligible if he or she remained married to the veteran until death and has not remarried.

- A divorced spouse is NOT eligible for pension benefits.*

Serving during one of the following periods of war considered by the VA is the second requirement.

- World War II: December 7, 1941 through December 31, 1946
- Korean War: June 27, 1950 through January 31, 1955
- Vietnam War: August 5, 1964 (February 28, 1961 for veterans who served in country before August 5, 1964) through May 7, 1975
- Gulf War: August 2, 1990 through a date to be set by law of Presidential Proclamation.**

This pension benefit is one of the most misunderstood benefits being administered by the VA today. There are veterans and spouses who are told that they do not qualify when in fact they can. There are a number of criteria that may affect your eligibility to pension benefits. Filing time is also important because all benefits are retro-dated back to the date that the VA receives the claim.

WHEN DO YOU NEED YOUR MONEY?

How long does your income need to last? Are there certain expenses you expect to crop up in the future such as health care costs? Are you expecting to inherit some money? Do you plan to liquidate assets such as a home or real estate property? Creating an income plan that lasts as long as you do requires careful planning for 10, 15, and sometimes even 30 years down the road. That's a lot of dollars. If you need your income to last you 10 years, you

---

*http://www.veteransaidbenefit.org/eligibility_aid_attendance_pension_benefit.htm
**http://benefits.va.gov/pension/wartimeperiod.asp

will want to use a tool that creates just that. If you need a lifetime of income, seek a tool that will do that and without running out.

So how do you figure out how much you need and when you need it? When you take health care costs, potential emergencies, plans for moving or traveling, and other retirement expenses into account, you can really give your calculator a workout. This is why Green Money becomes much more important as you age. While you want to reduce the amount of Red Money you have and to transition it to Green Money, you don't necessarily need all of it to generate income for you right away. You want to maximize retirement benefits to meet your lifetime income needs. Taking a closer look at Green Money, you will see there are actually different types.

TYPES OF GREEN MONEY:
NEED NOW AND NEED LATER

There are basically two types of Green Money: money used for income today and money used for accumulation to meet your income needs in five, 10 or 20 years. Money needed for income is Need Now Money. It is money you need to meet your basic needs, to pay your bills, your mortgage if you have one and the costs associated with maintaining your lifestyle. Money used for accumulation is Need Later Money. It's money that you don't need now for income, but will need to rely on down the road. It's still Green Money because you will rely on it later for income and will need to count on it being there. Need Later Money represents income your assets will need to generate for future use. When planning your retirement, it is vital to decide how much of your assets to structure for income and how much to set aside to accumulate to create Need Later Money.

You must figure out if your income and accumulation needs are met. Your Need Now and Need Later Money are top priorities. Need Now Money, in particular, will dictate what your options are for future needs such as planning for contingencies.

WHERE IS THIS MONEY COMING FROM?
INCOME THAT CAN'T BE CHANGED

The first place we look for income producing sources are Green Money options such as pensions and Social Security. The amount of income provided by those sources can't be changed and they provide the retirement base from which you build up from until you reach the number you need. An Investment Advisor can help you customize an income plan based on your current expenses and contingencies by utilizing a strategy that provides both Need Now and Need later money.

One kind of Green Money that most Americans can rely on for income when they retire is Social Security. If you're like most Americans, Social Security is or will be an important part of your retirement income and one that you should know how to properly manage. As a first step in creating your income plan, a financial professional will take a look at your Social Security benefit options. Social Security is the foundation of income planning for anyone who is about to retire today and is such a reliable source of Green Money in your overall income plan, we have dedicated the next chapter in this book to this one subject alone.

CHAPTER 3 RECAP //

- Outliving your money is what retirees fear the most. Build your retirement income from the sound foundation of Green Money, or Know So Money. The foundation of a retirement strategy depends on knowing how much money you need and when you need it.

- Identify how much of your income you Need Now, and how much you Need Later. Once you have your current Need Now income needs supplied, it's crucial to the longevity of your income to plan for Need Later Money. Unexpected expenses such as health care can devastate your nest egg if not planned for carefully.

- Statistics reveal that 65 percent of us will at some time require supervised care by a medical professional either at home, in a nursing home, or in an assisted care living facility.

- Conventional long term care insurance can be expensive but less so if purchased when you are young, and like any life insurance product, it can provide you with peace of mind.

- Some annuities and newer life insurance policies that specify a Living Benefit can provide the insuree with a stipend each month to help defray the costs of long term care. The benefit of a life insurance policy with a Living Benefit is that the policy will pay your beneficiaries when you die as well as paying you while you are still alive to help fund long term care.

- If you or your spouse is a war veteran, you may qualify for the Aid and Attendance. This benefit is designed to assist veteran or spouse paying out of pocket for long term care and is available to individuals who reside in assisted living communities, personal care homes, skilled nursing facilities and those receiving personal in-home care.

4

MAXIMIZING YOUR SOCIAL SECURITY BENEFIT

"Does it matter when I take my Social Security benefit?"

Lisa starting taking her Social Security benefit at the age of 62. This was the earliest time she could start receiving her benefit, and she thought she better go ahead and do it, after all, she was entitled to the money. Because she started taking the benefit at age 62, she received $750 a month instead of the $1,000 she would have received had she waited until FRA – her Full Retirement Age of 65. But Lisa didn't know this. She was busy working part-time so she could help pay for her son's college tuition. Lisa enjoyed her job well enough so it didn't seem like a huge sacrifice. Even with her reduced hours, she was still making $28,000 a year and it made her feel good to be earning a *little money. What she didn't realize, however, was that she was being penalized $1 for every $2 dollars that she earned over the amount of $15,480.* This cut her $750 Social Security benefit in half, so now instead of receiving $1,000 or $750, she was receiving only $375 a month.*

Two years later, Lisa is getting closer to retirement and so she attends a Social Security seminar with her friend, Judy. That night, Lisa is horrified to realize that she has made a big mistake. She didn't know about the penalties charged for withdrawing on her benefit while still working and she didn't know that her monthly benefit would have increased if only she had waited a few years longer. After the presentation, she approaches the financial professional who spoke during the seminar. She asked him, "Is there anything I can do to reverse this mistake? Can I stop taking my benefit now? And then take it again at a later date?" The financial professional had to tell her the bad news, "I'm sorry, but after the first year, the rate on your benefit is locked in for life."

In Lisa's case, her benefit will go back up to $750 a month once she stops working, but she will never be able to get the $1,000 a month she was entitled to at Full Retirement Age. Lisa was shortchanged due to lack of knowledge. For most people, working while claiming their Social Security benefit is a bad idea. Unless you have health considerations or are really in a financial pinch, it doesn't make sense to be paying out $1 for every $2 that you earn.

These penalties and other early withdrawal charges are designed by the Social Security administration to encourage retirees to keep working a little longer. The longer you work, the more money is paid into the system. There are other options such as File and Suspend and the Spousal Benefit, which might be able to increase your monthly benefit amount by a few hundred dollars. Whether

---

*http://www.ssa.gov/retire2/whileworking.htm

or not these strategies will benefit you depends on your individual situation. So, to whom should you turn for advice when making this complex decision? Before you pick up the phone and call Uncle Sam, you should know that the Social Security Administration (SSA) representatives are actually prohibited from giving you election advice! Plus, SSA representatives in general are trained to focus on monthly benefit amounts, not the lifetime income for a family.

As a first step in creating your income plan, ask your financial professional to take a look at your Social Security benefit options. The Social Security optimization report is not a product that can be sold, but rather is a service provided by many independent financial professionals. It doesn't put money into the pocket of your financial professional; it puts money into your pocket. Here are some facts that illustrate how Americans today currently use Social Security:

- 90 percent of Americans age 65 and older receive Social Security benefits.*
- Social Security provides 39 percent of income for retired Americans.*
- Claiming Social Security benefits at the wrong time can reduce your monthly benefit by up to 57 percent.**
- 43 percent of men and 48 percent of women claim Social Security benefits at age 62.**
- 74 percent of retirees receive reduced Social Security benefits.**
- In 2013, the average monthly Social Security benefit was $1,261. *The maximum benefit for 2013 was $2,533. The*

---

*http://www.ssa.gov/pressoffice/basicfact.htm

**When to Claim Social Security Benefits, David Blanchett, CFA, CFP® January, 2013

$1,272 monthly benefit reduction between the average and the maximum is applied for life.*

PENALTIES AND EARLY WITHDRAWAL CHARGES

For most people, there are three things you want to make sure you don't do unless life circumstances or health concerns dictate otherwise. The three biggest mistakes retirees make when claiming their Social Security benefit are: filing too early, filing while you are still working, and failing to take advantage of spousal benefits.

Filing too early: As was true for Lisa in the story above, taking your benefit at the earliest time possible, which is age 62, will cost you thousands of dollars over the course of your lifetime. The Social Security administration charges what amounts to an early withdrawal charge if you start claiming your benefit at age 62. Take your benefit then, and you will only receive 75 percent of your benefit amount.** And remember, this monthly benefit is locked in for the rest of your life once you elect to start taking the benefit. A person can change their Social Security election before the first year has lapsed as long as they do these two things: change it within the first 12 months of electing it, and pay back all of the benefits received.*** For example, if you're 62 ½, you would need to make the change before you reach age 63 ½. And you would have to pay back all of the benefits received during that first year. You are also only allowed one withdrawal per lifetime.

Filing while you are still working: the MAIN reason not to file for your Social Security benefit is if you are still going to keep working. While you are working, your earnings reduce your benefit amount until you reach your Full Retirement Age (FRA.) If you are under full retirement age for the entire year, you will be

---

*http://www.socialsecurity.gov/pressoffice/factsheets/colafacts2013.com

**http://www.ssa.gov/retire2/retirechart.htm

***http://www.ssa.gov/retire2/withdrawal.htm

penalized $1 from your benefit payments for every $2 you earn above the annual limit. The annual limit for 2014 is $15,480.* If you wait until after age 66 (FRA,) you can work as much as you want without penalty.

Failing to Take Advantage of Spousal Benefits: The Spousal Benefit is a monthly payment available to the spouse of someone who is eligible to receive Social Security. From an income planning standpoint, it could give a married couple an additional $12,000 a year in the budget, depending on their Primary Insurance Amount (PIA.) Many people do not know about this strategy and might be missing out on benefits they have earned.

There's a lot to know about Social Security. There are over 2,000 regulations and a number of benefits including pension pay-outs for persons caring for an adult disabled child, dependent parent or grandchild. These benefit amounts depend on the age of the child and other qualifications. Figuring out how to maximize your benefit is never as easy as people think. Experts spend their entire careers understanding and analyzing it. Luckily, you don't have to understand all of the intricacies of Social Security to maximize its advantages. You simply need to know the best way to manage *your* Social Security benefit. You need to know exactly what to do to get the most from your Social Security benefit and when to do it. Taking the time to create a roadmap for your Social Security strategy will help ensure that you are able to exact your maximum benefit and efficiently coordinate it with the rest of your retirement plan.

FOUR IMPORTANT STRATEGIES/BENEFITS

The Retired Worker Benefit is the benefit with which most people are familiar. It is what most people are talking about when they refer to Social Security. This is your benefit based on your earnings

---

*http://www.ssa.gov/retire2/whileworking.htm

and the amount that you have paid into the system over the span of your career. There are four other main benefits/strategies that most people aren't as familiar with. Learning a little about these benefits and strategies can help you know what questions to ask when working with your financial professional to maximize your Retired Worker Benefit.

1. *File and Suspend:* This concept allows you to file at age 66 (which is full retirement age) and suspend the benefit. This means your benefit amount will continue to roll up, or grow each year at a rate of 8 percent. Once you file and suspend, you can trigger the benefit any time you want, but after age 70, the benefit no longer grows. Waiting to claim your benefit allows you to receive a higher lifetime benefit, but if you have health concerns, this might not be a good option for you.

2. *Spousal Benefit:* The Spousal Benefit is available to the spouse of someone who is eligible for Retired Worker Benefits. This benefit can work in tandem with File and Suspend in what is known as a Restricted Application. There are two components here at play. First, the Spousal benefit dictates that a lower-earning spouse is eligible to receive up to 50 percent of their spouse's benefit without triggering their own benefit. For example, if your husband is eligible to receive $2,000 a month, you can File and Suspend and then claim the Spousal Benefit. Your own benefit continues to grow at the 8 percent rate. At the same time, you will receive 50 percent of your spouse's benefit, which in this case amounts to an extra check for $1,000 a month. It's like picking up an extra half loaf of bread without any effort. Your hubby still receives his $2,000, and your own benefit still continues to grow.

3. *Divorced Spouse:* If you have gone through a divorce and were married for at least 10 years, you might be eligible to

receive 50 percent of your former spouse's benefit, even if your former spouse doesn't file. There are a few qualifications that must be met before you can receive this benefit:
- You were married to your former spouse for at least 10 years.
- You are at least 62 years old.
- You are currently unmarried and thus not eligible for the Spousal Benefits mentioned above.
- You aren't entitled to a higher Social Security benefit on your own record.*

4. *Survivor Benefit:* This is another benefit specific to married couples. It allows the surviving spouse to receive the higher of the two benefits in the event of death. For example, if your wife is eligible to receive $3,000 a month and your benefit is only $1,000 a month, your income would drop significantly were your wife to pass away. The Survivor Benefit dictates that in the event of her death, you could elect the higher of the two benefits. Instead of only receiving $1,000 a month, you would receive $3,000. Many widows don't know about this benefit and are living near or in poverty due to lack of knowledge.

With all of the different options, strategies and benefits to choose from, you can see why filing for Social Security is more complicated than just mailing in the paperwork. Gathering the data and making yourself aware of all your different options isn't enough to know exactly what to do, however. On the one hand, you can knock yourself out trying to figure out which options are best for you and wondering if you made the best decision. On the other hand, you can work with a financial professional who uses customized software that takes all the variables of your specific

---

*http://www.ssa.gov/retire2/yourdivspouse.htm

situation into account and calculates your best option. You have tens of thousands of different options for filing for your Social Security benefit. If your spouse is a different age than you are, it nearly doubles the amount of options you have. This is far more complicated arithmetic than most people can do on their own. If you want a truly accurate understanding of when and how to file, you need someone who will ask you the right questions about your situation, someone who has access to specialized software that can crunch the numbers. The reality is that you need to work with a professional that can provide you with the sophisticated analysis of your situation that will help you make a truly informed decision.

HOW DO I MAXIMIZE MY LIFETIME BENEFIT?

There are many aspects of Social Security that you have no control over. You don't control how much you put into it, and you don't control what it's invested in or how the government manages it. However, you do control when and how you file for benefits. The real question about Social Security that you need to answer is, "When should I start taking Social Security?" While this is the all-important question, there are a couple of key pieces of information you need to track down first.

Before we get into a few calculations and strategies that can make all the difference, let's start by covering the basic information about Social Security which should give you an idea of where you stand. Just as the foundation of a house creates the stable platform for the rest of the framework to rest upon, your Social Security benefit is an important part of your overall retirement plan. The purpose of the information that follows is not to give an exhaustive explanation of how Social Security works, but to give you some tools and questions to start understanding how Social Security affects your retirement and how you can prepare for it.

Let's start with eligibility.

Eligibility. Understanding how and when you are eligible for Social Security benefits will help clarify what to expect when the time comes to claim them.

To receive retirement benefits from Social Security, you must earn eligibility. In almost all cases, Americans born after 1929 must earn 40 quarters of credit to be eligible to draw their Social Security retirement benefit. In 2013, a Social Security credit represents $1,160 earned in a calendar quarter. The number changes as it is indexed each year, but not drastically. In 2012, a credit represented $1,130. Four quarters of credit is the maximum number that can be earned each year. In 2013, an American would have had to earn at least $4,640 to accumulate four credits. In order to qualify for retirement benefits, you must have earned a minimum number of credits. Additionally, if you are at least 62 years old and have been married to a recipient of Social Security benefits for at least 12 months, you can choose to receive Spousal Benefits. Although 40 is the minimum number of credits required to begin drawing benefits, it is important to know that once you claim your Social Security benefit, there is no going back. Although there may be cost of living adjustments made, you are locked into that base benefit amount forever.

Primary Insurance Amount. You can think of your Primary Insurance Amount (PIA) like a ripening fruit. It represents the amount of your Social Security benefit at your Full Retirement Age (FRA). Your benefit becomes fully ripe at your FRA, and will neither reduce nor increase due to early or delayed retirement options. If you opt to take benefits before your FRA, however, your monthly benefit will be less than your PIA. You will essentially be picking an unripened fruit. On the one hand, waiting until after your FRA to access your benefits will increase your benefit beyond your PIA. On the other hand, you don't want the fruit to overripen, because every month you wait is one less check you get from the government.

Full Retirement Age. Your FRA is an important figure for anyone who is planning to rely on Social Security benefits in their retirement. Depending on when you were born, there is a specific age at which you will attain FRA. Your FRA is dictated by your year of birth and is the age at which you can begin your full monthly benefit. Your FRA is important because it is half of the equation used to calculate your Social Security benefit. The other half of the equation is based on when you start taking benefits.

When Social Security was initially set up, the FRA was age 65, and it still is for people born before 1938. But as time has passed, the age for receiving full retirement benefits has increased. If you were born between 1938 and 1960, your full retirement age is somewhere on a sliding scale between 65 and 67. Anyone born in 1960 or later will now have to wait until age 67 for full benefits. Increasing the FRA has helped the government reduce the cost of the Social Security program, which pays out more than a half trillion dollars to beneficiaries every year!*

While you can begin collecting benefits as early as age 62, the amount you receive as a monthly benefit will be less than it would be if you wait until you reached your FRA or surpass your FRA. It is important to note that if you file for Social Security benefit before your FRA, the reduction to your monthly benefit will remain in place for the rest of your life. You can also delay receiving benefits up to age 70, in which case your benefits will be higher than your PIA for the rest of your life.

- At FRA, 100 percent of PIA is available as a monthly benefit.
- At age 62, your Social Security retirement benefits are available. For each month you take benefits prior to your FRA, however, the monthly amount of your benefit is

---

*http://www.ssa.gov/pressoffice/basicfact.htm

reduced. This reduction stays in place for the rest of your life.

- At age 70, your monthly benefit reaches its maximum. After you turn age 70, your monthly benefit will no longer increase.

Year of Birth	Full Retirement Age
1943-1954	66
1955	66 and 2 months
1956	66 and 4 months
1957	66 and 6 months
1958	66 and 8 months
1959	66 and 10 months
1960 or later	age 67*

ROLLING UP YOUR SOCIAL SECURITY

Your Social Security income "rolls up" the longer you wait to claim it. Your monthly benefit will continue to increase until you turn 70 years old. But because Social Security is the foundation of most people's retirement, many Americans feel that they don't have control over how or when they receive their benefits. As a matter of fact, only 4 percent of Americans wait until after their FRA to file for benefits! This trend persists, despite the fact that every dollar you increase your Social Security income by means less money you will have to spend from your nest egg to meet your retirement income needs! For many people, creating their Social Security strategy is the most important decision they can make to positively impact their retirement. The difference between the best and worst Social Security decision can be tens of thousands of dollars over a lifetime of benefits — up to $170,000!

**http://www.ssa.gov/OACT/progdata/nra.html

WHEN IS THE BEST TIME TO START TAKING SOCIAL SECURITY?

Following the above logic, it makes sense to wait as long as you can to begin receiving your Social Security benefit. However, the answer isn't always that simple. Not everyone has the option of waiting. Many people need to rely on Social Security on day one of their retirement. In fact, **nearly 50 percent of 62-year-old Americans file for Social Security benefits.** Why is this number so high? Some might need the income. Others might be in poor health and don't feel they will live long enough to make FRA worthwhile for themselves or their families. It is also possible, however, that the majority of folks taking an early benefit at age 62 simply don't know any better.

File Immediately if You:
- Find your job is unbearable.
- Are willing to sacrifice retirement income.
- Are not healthy and need a reliable source of income.

Consider Delaying Your Benefit if You:
- Want to maximize your retirement income.
- Want to increase retirement benefits for your spouse.
- Are still working and like it.
- Are healthy and willing / able to wait to file.

So if you decide to wait, how long should you wait? Lots of people can put it off for a few years, but not everyone can wait until they are 70 years old. Your individual circumstances may be able to help you determine when you should begin taking Social Security. If you do the math, you will quickly see that between ages 62 and 70, there are 96 months in which you can file for your Social Security benefit. If you take into account those 96 months and the 96 months your spouse could also file for Social Security, the number of different strategies for structuring your benefit, you can easily end up with more than 20,000 different scenarios. It's safe to say this isn't the kind of math that most people can easily handle. Each month would result in a different benefit amount. The longer you wait, the higher your monthly benefit amount becomes. Each month you wait, however, is one less month that you receive a Social Security check.

The goal is to maximize your lifetime benefits. That may not always mean waiting until you can get the largest monthly payment. Taking the bigger picture into account, you want to find out how to get the most money out of Social Security over the number of years that you draw from it. Don't underestimate the power of optimizing your benefit: the difference between the BEST and WORST Social Security election can easily be between $30,000 to $50,000 in lifetime benefits. **The difference can be very substantial!**

If you know that every month you wait, your Social Security benefit goes up a little bit, and you also know that every month you wait, you receive one less benefit check, how do you determine where the sweet spot is that maximizes your benefits over your lifetime? Financial professionals have access to software that will calculate the best year and month for you to file for benefits based on your default life expectancy. You can further customize that information by estimating your life expectancy based on your health, habits and family history. If you can then create an income plan (we'll get into this later in the chapter) that helps you wait until the target date for you to file for Social Security, you can optimize your retirement income strategy to get the most out of your Social Security benefit. How can you calculate your life expectancy? Well, you don't know exactly how long you'll live, but you have a better idea than the government does. They rely on averages to make their calculations. **You have much more personal information about your health, lifestyle and family**

history than they do. You can use that knowledge to game the system and beat all the other people who are making uninformed decisions by filing early for Social Security.

While you can and should educate yourself about how Social Security works, the reality is you don't need to know a lot of general information about Social Security in order to make choices about your retirement. What you do need to know is exactly **what to do to maximize your benefit.** Because knowing what you need to do has a huge impact on your retirement! For most Americans, Social Security is the foundation of income planning for retirement. Social Security benefits represent nearly 40 percent of the income of retirees.* For many people, it can represent the largest portion of their retirement income. Not treating your Social Security benefit as an asset and investment tool can lead to sub-optimization of your largest source of retirement income.

Let's take a look at an example that shows the impact of working with a financial professional to optimize Social Security benefits:

> » *Richard and Lorraine Butler are a typical American couple who have worked their whole lives and saved when they could. Richard is 60 years old, and Lorraine is 56 years old. They sat down with a financial professional who logged onto the Social Security website to look up their PIAs. Richard's PIA is $1,900 and Lorraine's is $900.*
>
> *If the Butlers cash in at age 62 and begin taking retirement benefits from Social Security, they will receive an estimated $492,000 in lifetime benefits. That may seem like a lot, but if you divide that amount over 20 years, it averages out to be just shy of $25,000 per year. The Butlers are accustomed to a more significant annual income than that. To make up the difference, they will have to rely on alternative retirement*

---

*http://www.ssa.gov/pressoffice/basicfact.htm

income options. They will basically have to depend on a bigger nest egg to provide them with the income they need.

If they wait until their FRA, they will increase their lifetime benefits to an estimated $523,700. This option allows them to achieve their Primary Insurance Amount, which will provide them a $33,000 annual income.

After learning the Butlers' needs and using software to calculate the most optimal time to begin drawing benefits, the Butlers' financial professional determined that the best option for them drastically increases their potential lifetime benefits to $660,000!

By using strategies that their financial professional recommended, they increased their potential lifetime benefits by as much as $148,000. There's no telling how much you could miss out on from your Social Security if you don't take time to create a strategy that calculates your maximum benefit. For the Butlers, the value of maximizing their benefits was the difference between night and day. While this may seem like a special case, it isn't uncommon to find benefit increases of this magnitude. You'll never know unless you take a look at your own options.

Despite the importance of knowing when and how to take your Social Security benefit, many of today's retirees and pre-retirees may know little about the mechanics of Social Security and how they can maximize their benefit.

MAXIMIZING YOUR LIFETIME BENEFIT
As discussed in Chapter 2, calculating how to maximize lifetime benefits is more important than waiting until age 70 for your maximum monthly benefit amount. It's about getting the most income during your lifetime. Professional benefit maximization

software can target the year and month that it is most beneficial for you to file based on your life expectancy.

The three most common ages that people associate with retirement benefits are 62 (Earliest Eligible Age), 66 (Full Retirement Age), and 70 (age at which monthly maximum benefit is reached). In almost all circumstances, however, none of those three most common ages will give you the maximum lifetime benefit.

Remember, every month you wait to file, the amount of your benefit check goes up, but you also get one less check. You don't know exactly how long you're going to live, but you have a better idea of your life expectancy than the actuaries at the Social Security Administration who can only work with averages. They can't make calculations based on your specific situation. A professional can run the numbers for you and get the target date that maximizes your potential lifetime benefits. You can't get this information from the SSA, but you **can** get it from a financial professional.

Your Social Security options don't stop here, however. There are a plethora of other choices you can make to manipulate your benefit payments.

Important Questions about Your Social Security Benefit:
- How can I maximize my lifetime benefit? By knowing when and how to file for Social Security. This usually means waiting until you have at least reached your Full Retirement Age. A professional has the experience and the tools to help determine when and how you can maximize your lifetime benefits.
- Who will provide reliable advice for making these decisions? Only a professional has the tools and experience to provide you reliable advice.
- Will the Social Security Administration provide me with the advice? The Social Security Administration cannot

provide you with advice or strategies for claiming your benefit. They can give you information about your monthly benefit, but that's it. They also don't have the tools to tell you what your specific best option is. They can accurately answer how the system works, but they can't advise you on what decision to make as to how and when to file for benefits.

The Maximization Report that your financial professional will generate represents an invaluable resource for understanding how and when to file for your Social Security benefit. When you get your customized Social Security Maximization Report, you will not only know all the options available to you – but you will understand the financial implications of each choice. In addition to the analysis, you will also get a report that shows *exactly* at what age – including which month and year – you should trigger benefits and how you should apply. It also includes a variety of other time-specific recommendations, such as when to apply for Medicare or take Required Minimum Distributions from your qualified plans. A report means there is no need to wonder, or to try to figure out when to take action – the Social Security Maximization Report lays it all out for you in plain English.

CHAPTER 4 RECAP //

- Working while taking your Social Security benefit causes you to be penalized $1 for every $2 you make over $15,480 as of 2014. Claiming your Social Security at age 62 also reduces your benefit by 25 percent.

- You cannot get advice about how to maximize your lifetime benefit from a Social Security representative. They are prohibited from giving advice about when to elect your benefit options.

- The three biggest mistakes people make when filing for Social Security are: filing too early, filing while still working and failing to take advantage of Spousal Benefits.

- The four main strategies/benefits of which you need to be knowledgeable are: File and Suspend, the Spousal Benefit, benefits for a Divorced Spouse, and the Survivor Benefit.

- To get the most out of your Social Security benefit, you need to file at the right time. Every dollar your Social Security income increases is less money you'll have to spend from your retirement savings to supplement your income. An Investment Advisor can help you determine when you should file for Social Security to get your Maximum Lifetime Benefit.

- Deciding when to take your Social Security benefit is one of the most important decisions you make as a retiree. After the first year of taking the benefit, that amount is locked in for the duration of your lifetime.

- If you change your mind about when you wish to receive your Social Security benefit, you have the option to cancel as long as you do it within the first year of receiving benefits and pay back the full dollar amount of all benefits received.

5

NEW TOOLS TO FILL
THE INCOME GAP

"Why hasn't anybody told me about this?"

Dennis and Lavone are 62 years old and have decided to run the numbers to see what their retirement is going to look like. They know they currently need $6,000 per month to pay their bills and maintain their current lifestyle. They have also done their Social Security homework and have determined that, between the two of them, they will receive $4,200 per month in benefits. They also receive $350 per month in rent from a tenant who lives in a small carriage house in their backyard. Between their Social Security and the monthly rent income, they will be short $1,450 per month.

They do have an additional asset, however. Dennis has been contributing for years to an IRA that has reached a value of $350,000.

They realize that they have to figure out how to turn the $350,000 in the IRA into $1,450 per month for the rest of their lives.

At first glance, it may seem like they will have plenty of money. With some quick calculations, they find they have 240 months, or nearly 20 years, of monthly income before they exhaust the account. When you consider income tax, the potential for higher taxes in the future, and market fluctuations (because many IRAs are invested in the market), the amount in the IRA seems to have a little less clout. Every dollar Dennis and Lavone take out of the IRA is subject to income tax, and if they leave the remainder in the IRA, they run the risk of losing money in a volatile market. Once they retire and stop getting a paycheck every two weeks, Dennis also stops contributing to the IRA. And when they aren't supplementing its growth with their own money, they are entirely dependent on market growth. That's a scary prospect. They could also withdraw the money from the IRA and put it in a savings account or CD, but removing all the money at once will put them in a tax bracket that will claim a huge portion of the value of the IRA. A seemingly straightforward asset has now become a complicated equation. Dennis and Lavone don't know what to do.

After you have calculated your Social Security benefit and have selected the year and month that will maximize your lifetime benefits, you will likely need to find another source of income in order to keep the lifestyle you have grown accustomed to. It's time to look at your other retirement assets, incomes and options that can help fill in your monthly income needs. Like Dennis and Lavone, you may have a pension, an IRA or Roth IRA, dividends from stock holdings, money from the sale of real estate, rental property, or other sources of income. But how can these assets be structured so as to provide a protected, guaranteed income stream that grows enough to keep up with inflation and taxes?

WILL YOU HAVE ENOUGH MONEY?

The moment that you stop working and start living off the money that you've set aside for retirement can be referred to as the Retirement Cliff. You've worked and earned money your whole life, but the day that you retire, that income comes to an end. That's the day that you have to have other assets that fill the gap. Social Security will fill in some, but you need to come up with something else. After you have calculated your Social Security benefit and have selected the year and month that will maximize your lifetime benefits, it's time to look at your other retirement assets that will reduce or eliminate the drop-off of the Retirement Cliff.

If your monthly Social Security check and your other supplemental income leaves a shortfall in your desired income, how are you going to fix it? This shortfall is called the Income Gap and it needs to be filled in order to maintain your lifestyle into retirement. If you have a known income gap that you need to fill, you want to know how to fill that income gap with the fewest dollars possible. You don't want it to cost you too much, because you want to get the most out of your other assets, including planning for your future and planning for your legacy. You do that by maximizing your Social Security benefit, leveraging your additional income and looking at other investment tools that can help generate income for you. Your specific needs, of course, should be analyzed by a professional.

DIFFERENT TYPES OF ANNUITIES AND WHAT THEY CAN DO

When you retire, you go from the accumulation phase of your life to what's known as the pay-out phase. The word annuity is defined as the annual payment of an allowance or income. The problem, however, is that the word annuity for a lot of people has negative connotations. If you have heard bad things about annuities in the past, it's usually the result of one particular culprit known as a Variable Annuity. We will talk about these so you understand how they work and how they are different from the new annuities of today.

Today's annuities have been designed to solve problems specific to today's retirees. They work very much like Social Security in that they give you that reliable pension check every month, but that's not all they can do. A long term care rider can also be added to your annuity at the time of its purchase. Adding a long term care rider can provide you or your spouse with an income doubler should one of you need to fund the cost of long term care during your lifetime. A linked benefit is another word for a long term care benefit, also known as Living Benefits. Living Benefits provide you with money while you are still alive to cover the expense of home health care and long term care. Annuities are a life insurance product and there are many different kinds of annuities you can purchase to fill your income gap and address other income concerns.

Ask yourself the following questions:

- How concerned are you about finding a secure financial vehicle to protect your savings?
- How concerned are you that there may be a better way to structure your savings?

It's not about whether the market goes up or down, but when it does. If it goes down at the wrong time for your five or 10 year retirement horizon, you could be in serious danger of losing some of your retirement income. If you are concerned about the best way to fill your income gap, one or more of these annuities working alone or together might be the right investment tool for you.

Fixed Indexed Annuities (FIAs) are such a specialized type of annuity once referred to as Equity Indexed Annuities, or EIAs. The key to how well these annuities perform has to do with a strategy known as indexing. The annuity is keyed to an equity index such as the S&P 500 so it can mirror the performance of that index, without participating directly in the equity investment. These annuities can offer the income dependability of a pension controlled and administered by you. You choose the amount of money you put in, when to turn on the income stream, and for how long. They offer a guarantee of principal, grow money on a tax-deferred basis and offer lifetime income options.

Variable annuities can lose money due to market fluctuations. As their name suggests, they vary with the stock market and the value of the principal is not guaranteed. If you have heard rotten things about annuities, it was most likely a variable annuity product. If you purchase an income rider on a variable annuity, the Income Account Value will stay the same, but the value of your *actual* contract may fall. If you surrender the annuity, the insurance company will pay you the market value of the asset, regardless of whether it matches, exceeds or falls short of the value at which you bought the contract. If its value has dropped significantly, you may be better off taking the income rider as an income-for-life stream without surrendering your contract.

Single Premium Immediate Annuities (SPIAs) are structured so that you pay a lump sum of money (a single premium) to an insurance company, and they give you a guaranteed income over an agreed upon time period. That time period could be five years, or it could be for the remainder of your lifetime. Guarantees from insurance companies are based on the claims-paying ability of the issuing insurance company.

SPIAs provide investors with a stream of reliable income when they can't afford to take the risk of losing money in a fluctuating market. While there is general faith that the market always trends up, at least in the long-term, if you are focusing on income over a shorter period of time, you may not be able to take a big hit in the market. Beyond normal market volatility, interest rates also come with an inherent level of uncertainty, making it hard to create a dependable income on your own. SPIAs reduce risk for you by giving you regular monthly, quarterly or yearly payments that can begin the moment you buy the contract. Your financial professional can walk you through a series of different payment options to help you select the one that most closely fits your needs.

In its simplest form, an annuity offers a way to invest money that allows you to structure it for income. Because there are so many different kinds of annuities with specific features, finding the right one for you will take a conversation with your financial professional. It's also possible to put more than one annuity product together in what is known as laddering strategy. Doing this can structure income for 5, 10 and 15 years down the road and provide for your Need Later Money needs. You can also use the laddering strategy while purchasing several annuities from more than one life insurance company. Annuities are based on the claims paying ability of the insurance company, so the ratings of the insurance company are important to investigate.

HOW TO WRITE YOURSELF A PENSION

When you put your money into an annuity, you are essentially buying an investment product from an insurance company. It is a contract between you and the insurance company that provides the investment tool. Let's say you have saved $100,000 and need it to generate income to meet your needs above and beyond your Social Security and pension checks. You give the $100,000 to an insurance company, who in turn invests it to generate growth.

They usually select investments that have modest returns over long term horizons. In other words, they generally put it somewhere stable and predictable. Most commonly, they will invest it in a combination of bonds and treasuries that are safer and dependable ways to grow money. They use the money from the insurance products they sell to invest, use a portion of the returns to generate profits for themselves, and return a portion to clients in the form of payouts, claims, and structured income options.

One of the most attractive qualities of these types of annuities is something called annual reset. Annual reset is sometimes also referred to as a "ratcheting." It works like this: If the market goes down, you don't suffer a loss. Instead, the insurance company absorbs it. But if the market goes up, you share with the insurance company some of the profit made on the gain. The amount of gain you get is called your annuity participation rate. Typically the insurer will cap the amount of gain you can realize at somewhere between 3 and 7 percent. If the market goes up 10 percent, you would realize a portion of that gain (whatever percentage you are capped at). This means you to never lose money on your investment, while always gaining a portion of the upswings. The measurement period of your annuity can be calculated monthly, weekly and even daily, but most annuities are measured annually. The level of the index when you buy and the index level one year later will determine the amount of loss or gain. You and the insurance company are betting that the market will generally go up over time.

HOW INCOME RIDERS WORK

When you use that $100,000 to buy a contract with an insurance company in the form of an annuity, you are pegging your money on an index. It could be the S&P 500, the Dow Jones Industrial Average or any number of indexes. To generate income from the annuity, you select something called an income rider. An income rider is a subset of an indexed annuity. Essentially, it is the amount of money from which the insurance company will pay you an income while you have your money in their annuity. Your income rider is a larger number than what your investment is actually worth, and if you select the income rider, it will increase in value over time, providing you with more income. As the insurance company holds your money and invests it, they generate a return on it that they use to pay you a regular monthly income based on a higher number. The insurance company has to outperform the amount that they pay you in order to make a profit.

Remember, insurance companies make long-term investments that provide them with predictable flows of money. They like to stabilize the amount of money that goes in and out of their doors instead of paying and receiving large unpredictable chunks at once. When you opt for an income rider, an insurance company can reliably predict how much money they will pay out to you over a set period of time. It's predictable, and they like that. They can base their business on those predictable numbers.

In order to encourage investors to leave their money in their annuity contracts, insurance companies create surrender periods that protect their investments. If you remove your money from the annuity contract during the surrender period, you will pay a penalty and will not be able to receive your entire investment amount back. A typical surrender period is 10 years. If after three years you decide that you want your $100,000 back, the insurance company has that money tied up in bonds and other investments with the understanding that they will have it for another seven years. Because they will take a hit on removing the money from their investments prematurely, you will have to pay a surrender charge that makes up for their loss. During the surrender period, an annuity is not a demand deposit account like a savings or checking account. The higher returns that you are guaranteed from an annuity are dependent on the timeframe you selected. The longer an insurance company can hold your money, the easier it is for them to guarantee a predictable return on it.

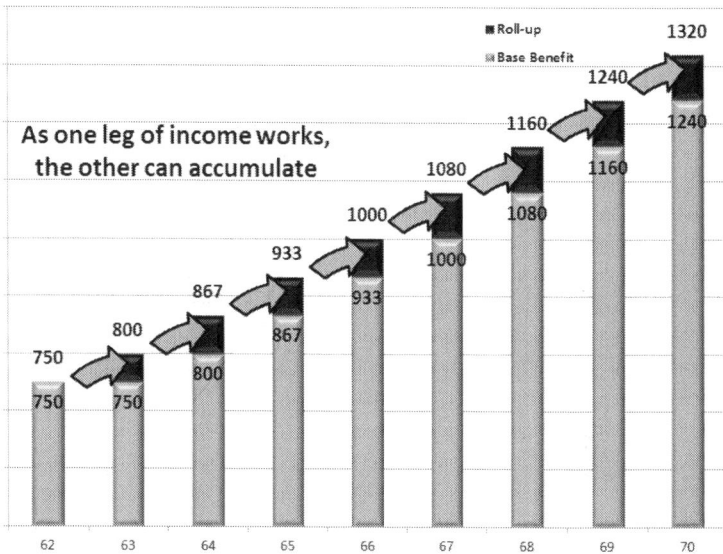

As one leg of income works,
the other can accumulate

■ Roll-up
▣ Base Benefit

This is a hypothetical illustration

If you leave your money in the annuity contract, you get a reliable monthly income no matter what happens in the market. Once the surrender period has expired, you can remove your money whenever you want. Your money becomes liquid again because the insurance company has used it in an investment that fit the timeline of your surrender period. For many people, this is an attractive trade off that can provide a creative solution for filling their income gap.

CRITICAL CARE RIDERS AND OTHER OPTIONS

As mentioned earlier, many life insurance products today also offer attractive options for funding the costs of long term care. Annuity products with critical care riders or penalty-free options for healthcare expenses can be important financial tools in the design of a good income plan. Some of these policies will let you access the money designated for your beneficiaries (known as a Death Benefit) to help take care of your long term care expenses now, while you are still alive. This is what's known as a Living Benefit.

On annuities, features such as this are known as health care riders. If you or your spouse meets certain qualifications due to a chronic illness or disability, that monthly income on your rider can be doubled. This means instead of receiving $1,500 a month, you will receive $3,000. This is what's known as an income doubler and it can provide the means necessary to pay additional medical expenses should you need some type of long term care.

When is an annuity with an income rider right for you? A good financial professional can help you make that determination by taking the time to listen closely to your situation and understanding what your needs are as you enter retirement. Every salesperson has a bag full of brochures and PowerPoint presentations, but they need to know exactly what the financial concerns of their individual clients are in order to help them make the most informed and beneficial decision. Some people need income today, others need it in five or 10 years. Others may have their income needs met but need help planning for those unknown contingencies coming down the road. If you want income in 15 years, you might want to choose a different investment product for 10 years, and then switch to an annuity with an income rider during the last five years of your timeline. Everyone's situation is different and everyone's needs are different.

Additional Annuity Information:
- Some contracts will allow you to draw income from the high water mark that the market reaches each year. The income rider will then begin calculating its value from the high water mark.

- Income annuities are investment tools that look and feel a bit like Social Security. Every year you allow the money to grow with the market, and it will "roll up" by a specific amount, paying out a specific percent to you as income each year.
- Annuities can work very well to create income, and a financial professional can help you find the one that best matches your income need, and can also structure it to work perfectly for you.
- If you are 68 years old and you have more immediate income needs that you need to come up with above and beyond your Social Security, you need a low risk, reliable source of income. If you choose an annuity option, you are looking for something that will pay out an income right away over a relatively short timeframe. You probably want to opt for a SPIA that pays you immediately and spans a five year period, as well as an additional annuity that begins paying you in five years, and another longer term annuity that begins paying you in 10 years. Bear in mind that each annuity contract has its own costs and fees. Review these with your financial professional before you determine the best products and strategies for your situation.

A GUARANTEED INCOME AND ACCUMULATION STRATEGY

The following example shows just how helpful an indexed annuity option can be for a retiree:

> *Bianca is 60 years old and is wondering how she can use her assets to provide her with a retirement income. She has a $5,000 per month income need. If she starts withdrawing her Social Security benefit in six years at age 66, it will provide*

her with $2,200 per month. She also has a pension that kicks in at age 70 that will give her another $1,320 per month.

That leaves an income gap of $2,800 from ages 66 to 69, and then an income gap of $1,480 at age 70 and beyond. If Bianca uses only Green Money to solve her income need, she will need to deposit $918,360 at 2 percent interest to meet her monthly goal for her lifetime. If she opts to use Red Money and withdraws the amount she needs each month from the market, let's say the S & P 500, she will run out of cash in 10 years if she invested between the years of 2000 and 2012. Suffering a market downturn like that during the period for which she is relying on it for retirement income will change her life, and not for the better.

Working with a financial professional to find a better way, Bianca found that she could take a hybrid approach to fill her income gap. Her professional recommended two different income vehicles: one that allowed her to deposit just $190,161 with a 2 percent return, and one that was a $146,000 income annuity. These tools filled her income gap with $336,161, requiring her to spend $582,000 less money to accomplish her goal! Working with a professional to find the right tools for her retirement needs saved Bianca over half a million dollars.

Creating an income plan before you retire allows you to satisfy your need for lifetime income and ensures that your lifestyle can last as long as you do. You also want to create a plan that operates in the most efficient way possible. Doing so will give more security to your Need Later Money and will potentially allow you to build your legacy down the road.

Yesterday's investment rules may not work today. Not only could they hamper achieving your goals, they may actually harm your financial situation. We are currently in a period when the rates for Know So Money options are at historic lows, and the volatility of Hope So Money is higher than ever. There is no overlapping acceptable rate, making both options less than ideal. *Because of this uncertain financial landscape, wise investment strategies are more important now than ever.*

Writing your own pension includes the following steps:
- Review your income needs and look specifically at the shortfall you may have during each year of your retirement based on your Social Security income, and income from any other assets you have.
- Ask yourself where you are in your distribution phase. Is retirement one year away? 10 years away? Last year?
- Determine how much money you need and how you need to structure your existing assets to provide for that need.
- If you have an asset from which you need to generate income, consider options offered by purchasing an income rider on an annuity.

» *Joni wants to retire at age 68. However, after her Social Security benefit, she will need nearly $375,000 in assets to generate a modest $40,000 of income per year.*

Amazingly, most people don't look ahead to think that at 68 years old, they will need $375,000 to have a basic lifestyle that pays out around $40,000 with Social Security benefits.

CHAPTER 5 RECAP //

- After Social Security and your additional income is accounted for, the amount that's left to meet your needs is called the *Income Gap*. It's important to consider future expense when planning for your income needs because most retirees will live longer than their parents did.
- Many retirees struggle to find the right investment tools during their retirement years. In the past, annuities have gotten some bad press so many people don't like the sound of the word, annuity. Today's annuities are designed to provide a guaranteed income and solve many of the problems faced by today's retirees.
- Typical interest rates on Green Money assets don't earn enough to keep pace with inflation and taxes, while money left in the market can potentially devastate your retirement income. Today's new annuities are designed to protect your retirement savings in any market.
- Although an annuity is an income-producing asset that does not subject your income to market risk, it still has the opportunity to grow. An FIA (Fixed Indexed Annuity), previously known as an EIA or Equity Indexed Annuity, is a special type of annuity that is keyed to the performance of the stock market. It offers growth with the guaranteed safety of your principal.
- The benefits of an FIA include: guarantee of principal, a minimum guaranteed cash value, no fees, access to your money, additional interest, tax deferral, and a guaranteed lifetime income.
- Be sure you understand the features, benefits, costs and fees associated with any annuity product before you invest.

6

IS THE MARKET RIGHT
FOR YOU DURING
RETIREMENT?

"Should I protect my retirement savings?"

Mary worked for a restaurant supply and distribution company for 34 years. During her time there, she acquired bonuses and pay raises that often included shares of stock in the company. She also dedicated part of her paycheck every month to a 401(k) that bought stock in the company. By the time she retired, Mary has $250,000 worth of company stock.

Although she had contributed to her 401(k) account every month, Mary didn't cultivate any other assets that could generate income for her during retirement. Mary also retired early at age 62 because of her failing health. The commute to work every day was becoming difficult in her weakened condition and she wanted to enjoy the rest of her life in retirement instead of working in the cramped office of the restaurant supply company.

Because she retired early, Mary failed to maximize her Social Security benefit. While she lives a modest lifestyle, her income needs are $3,500 per month. Mary's monthly Social Security check only covers $1,900, leaving her with a $1,600 income gap. To supplement her Social Security check, Mary sells $1,600 of company stock each month to meet her income needs. A $250,000 401(k) is nothing to sneeze at, but reducing its value by $1,600 every month will decimate her savings within 10 years. And that's if the market stays neutral or grows modestly. If the market takes a downturn, the money that Mary relies on to fill her income gap will rapidly diminish. Even if the market starts going up in a couple of years, it will take much larger gains for her to recover the value that she lost due to the math of rebounds (which will be explained shortly).

Unhappily for Mary, she retired in 2007, just before the major market downturn that lasted for several years. She lost more than 20 percent of the value of her stock. Because Mary needed to sell her stock to meet her basic income needs, the market price of the stock was secondary to her need for the money. When she needed money, she was forced to sell however many shares she needed to fill her income gap that month. And if she has a financial crisis, involving a need for long term medical care, for example, she will be forced to sell stock even if the market is low and her shares are nearly worthless. Mary realizes that she could have relied on an investment structured to deliver her a regular income while protecting the value of her investment. She could have kept her $250,000 from diminishing while enjoying her lifestyle into retirement regardless of the volatility of the market. Ideally, Mary would have restructured her 401(k) to reflect the level of risk that she was able to take. In her case, she would have had most of her money in a Know So Money assets, allowing her to rely on the value of her assets when she needed them.

It can be challenging to watch the stock market's erratic changes every month, week or even every day. When you have the security of your retirement income riding on it, the ride can feel pretty bumpy. Should you stay in the market and re-grow your assets, or get out now and move your money to safer investment vehicles? Knowing your timeline and understanding a few basic principles about stock market investing can help you make a more informed decision.

YOUR TIMELINE AND HOW MONEY GROWS

Taking a hit in the market hurts no matter how stable your income, but most people don't realize that it requires an even larger step forward to return to where you were once you take that step back. You might have the sentiment, "the market always comes back," but even if you do get back to where you were before the loss, your money isn't growing and earning the same way it was before the hit occurred. The *math of rebounds*, as it is known, uses the percentage of the investment, and not the dollar amount, to calculate what you will need to earn in order to recapture your loses.

For example, if you had $100,000 invested in the stock market in 2007, and along comes the downturn of 2008, the market takes a reduction of 50 percent. So now your $100,000 becomes $50,000. What has to happen for us to get back up to $100,000? It took a 50 percent loss to lose $50,000 but it will take a 100-percent gain to get your account back to where you were before. What this means for the average Joe and Mary is that it takes a LONG time to dig out of the hole.

Another thing most investors fail to consider when retiring is something known as the *sequence of returns*. The sequence of returns tells us that in addition to how the market performs, it is the order of those returns that are just as important when it comes to calculating the return value of our investments. The years just before and after you retire are especially crucial. Taking a loss during those years could significantly reduce the amount of your retirement nest egg for the long term. Consider the following example:

> » *Jack and Jill retired in 1995. They had $500,000 invested in stocks in the S&P 500, and are taking out $25,000, or 5 percent per year, to supplement their retirement income. The value of their account at the end of the year 2013 was $1,200,000. Their neighbors, Fred and Ethel are a few years younger, and they retired in the year 2000. They did exactly the same thing as Jack and Jill, withdrawing $25,000 per year from a $500,000 investment held in the stock market. The value of their account at the end of the year 2013 was $94,000.* *

This huge discrepancy is due to the sequence of returns. The only thing Fred and Ethel did differently was to retire five years later, yet that made a big difference in how their gains were calculated. During the first three years of their retirement, they took three big hits, while in the case of Jack and Jill, those same three big hits were calculated in the middle of the 13-year period as opposed to at the beginning. How will your gains be calculated? Well that all depends on how the market performs, and the order in which it performs. You may have the same $500,000 as a starting principal, with an average inflation rate of 3 percent and an average rate of

---

*This hypothetical example is for illustrative purposes only and is not a prediction or guarantee of actual results which will vary from those described. This example isn't intended to represent the value or performance of a specific product. The retirement vehicle in this example is assumed to be tax-deferred, so taxes are not paid until withdrawals are made. Annual withdrawals do not reflect the impact of taxes or inflation. Some retirement vehicles have charges, fees or expenses which are not reflected and which would lower the amounts available for withdrawal.

return at 8.43 percent, but it is the sequence of returns and your individual timeline that dictates what your final balance will be.

HOW REAL PEOPLE MAKE INVESTMENT DECISIONS

When you are managing your money by yourself, emotions inevitably enter into the mix. The Dow Jones Industrial Average and the S&P 500 represent more to you than market fluctuations. They represent a portion of your retirement. It's hard not to be emotional about it.

Everyone knows you should buy low and sell high. But what is more likely to happen has been well-documented in the following report:

In 2013, DALBAR, the well-respected financial services market research firm, released their annual "Quantitative Analysis of Investment Behavior" report (QAIB). The report studied the impact of market volatility on individual investors: people like Mary, or anyone who was managing (or mismanaging) their own investments in the stock market.

According to the study, volatility not only caused investors to make decisions based on their emotions, those decisions also harmed their investments and prevented them from realizing potential gains. So why do people meddle so much with their investments when the market is fluctuating? Part of the reason is that many people have financial obligations that they don't have control over. Significant expenses like house payments, the unexpected cost of replacing a broken-down car, and medical bills can put people in a position where they need money. If they need to sell investments to come up with that money, they don't have the luxury of selling when they *want* to. They must sell when they *need* to.

DALBAR's "Quantitative Analysis of Investor Behavior" has been used to measure the effects of investors' buying, selling and mutual fund switching decisions since 1994. The QAIB shows time and time again over nearly a 20 year period that the average investor earns less, and in many cases, significantly less than the performance of mutual funds suggests. QAIB's goal is to improve independent investor performance and to help financial professionals provide helpful advice and investment strategies that address the concerns and behaviors of the average investor.

An excerpt from the report claims that:

"QAIB offers guidance on how and where investor behaviors can be improved. No matter what the state of the mutual fund industry, boom or bust: Investment results are more dependent on investor behavior than on fund performance. Mutual fund investors who hold on to their investments are more successful than those who time the market.

QAIB uses data from the Investment Company Institute (ICI), Standard & Poor's and Barclays

Capital Index Products to compare mutual fund investor returns to an appropriate set of benchmarks.

There are actually three primary causes for the chronic shortfall for both equity and fixed income investors:

1. *Capital not available to invest. This accounts for 25 percent to 35 percent of the shortfall.*
2. *Capital needed for other purposes. This accounts for 35 percent to 45 percent of the shortfall.*
3. *Psychological factors. These account for 45 percent to 55 percent of the shortfall."*

The key findings of Dalbar's QAIB report provide compelling statistics about how individual investment strategies produced negative outcomes for the majority of investors:

- Psychological factors account for 45 percent to 55 percent of the chronic investment return shortfall for both equity and fixed income investors.

- Asset allocation is designed to handle the investment decision-making for the investor, which can materially reduce the shortfall due to psychological factors.
- Successful asset allocation investing requires investors to act on two critical imperatives:
    1. Balance capital preservation and appreciation so that they are aligned with the investor's objective.
    2. Select a qualified allocator.
- The best way for an investor to determine their risk tolerance is to utilize a risk tolerance assessment. However, these assessments must be accessible and usable.
- Evaluating allocator quality requires analysis of the allocator's underlying investments, decision making process and whether or not past efforts have produced successful outcomes.
- Choosing a top allocator makes a significant difference in the investment results one will achieve.
- Mutual fund retention rates suggest that the average investor has not remained invested for long enough periods to derive the potential benefits of the investment markets.
- Retention rates for asset allocation funds exceed those of equity and fixed income funds by over a year.
- Investors' ability to correctly time the market is highly dependent on the direction of the market. Investors generally guess right more often in up markets. However, in 2012 investors guessed right only 42 percent of the time during a bull market.
- Analysis of investor fund flows compared to market performance further supports the argument that investors are unsuccessful at timing the market. Market upswings rarely coincide with mutual fund inflows while market downturns do not coincide with mutual fund outflows.

- Average equity mutual fund investors gained 15.56 percent compared to a gain of 15.98 percent that just holding the S&P 500 produced.
- The shortfall in the long-term annualized return of the average mutual fund equity investor and the S&P 500 continued to decrease in 2012.
- The fixed-income investor experienced a return of 4.68 percent compared to an advance of 4.21 percent on the Barclays Aggregate Bond Index.
- The average fixed income investor has failed to keep up with inflation in nine out of the last 14 years.*

It doesn't take a financial services market research report to tell you that market volatility is out of your control. The report does prove, however, that before you experience market volatility, you should have an investment plan, and when the market is fluctuating, you should stand by your plan. This harkens back to the story at the beginning of the book, when Mr. and Mrs. Jones were flying an airplane that developed a fuel leak. When the stock market takes a downturn, the dollars you've worked so hard to save begin leaking out of your account. It's natural to have an emotional reaction to that, and do one of two things: react like a deer-in-the-headlights and do nothing, keeping everything as is; or, jump ship, leap from the plan, sell your stocks and get out while you can. Having a plan helps to steady the emotions of bad news during turbulent times.

You should review and discuss your investment plan with your financial professional on a regular basis, ensuring he/she is aware of any changes in your goals, financial circumstances, your health or your risk tolerance. When the economy is under stress and the markets are volatile, investors can feel vulnerable. That vulnerability causes people to tinker with their portfolios in an

---

2013 QAIB, Dalbar, March 2013

attempt to outsmart the market. Financial professionals, however, don't try to time the market for their clients. They have the ability to remain un-emotional when it comes to your money, and are better able to make decisions based on the numbers, and not those emotions. Using these numbers as their guide, they can tap into the gains that can be realized by committing to long-term investment strategies.

SEEKING FINANCIAL ADVICE: STOCK BROKERS VS. INVESTMENT ADVISOR REPRESENTATIVES

Investors basically have access to two types of advice in today's financial world: advice from stock brokers and advice given by investment advisors. Most investors, however, don't know the difference between types of advice and the people from whom they receive advice. Today, there are two primary types of advice offered to investors: advice given by a commission-based registered representative (brokers) and advice given by fee-based Investment Advisor Representatives. Unfortunately, many investors are not aware that a difference exists; nor have they been explained the distinction between the two types of advice. In a survey taken by TD Ameritrade, the top reasons investors choose to work with an independent registered investment advisor are:*

- Registered Investment Advisors are required, as fiduciaries, to offer advice that is in the best interest of clients
- More personalized service and competitive fee structure offered at a Registered Investment Advisor firm
- Dissatisfaction with full commission brokers

The truth is that there is a great deal of difference between stock brokers and investment advisor representatives. For starters,

---

*2011 Advisor Sentiment Study, commissioned by TD AMERITRADE. TD Ameritrade, Inc.

investment advisor representatives are obligated to act in an investor's best interests in all aspects of a financial relationship. Confusion continues to exist among investors struggling to find the best financial advice out there and the most credible sources of advice.

Here is some information to help clear up the confusion so you can find good advice from a professional you can trust:

- Investment advisor representatives have the fiduciary duty to act in a client's best interest at all times with every investment decision they make. Stock brokers and brokerage firms usually do not act as fiduciaries to their investors and are not obligated to make decisions that are entirely in the best interest of their customers. For example, if you decide you want to invest in precious metals, a stock broker would offer you a precious metals account from their firm. An Investment Advisor would find you a precious metals account that is the best fit for you based on the investment strategy of your portfolio.
- Investment advisors give their clients a Form ADV describing the methods that the professional uses to do business. An Investment Advisor also obtains client consent regarding any conflicts of interest that could exist with the business of the professional.
- Stock brokers and brokerage firms are not obligated to provide comparable types of disclosure to their customers.
- Whereas stock brokers and firms routinely earn large profits by trading as principal with customers, Investment Advisors cannot trade with clients as principal (except in very limited and specific circumstances).
- Investment Advisors charge a pre-negotiated fee with their clients in advance of any transactions. They cannot earn additional profits or commissions from their customers' investments without prior consent. Registered Investment

Advisors are commonly paid an asset-based fee that aligns their interests with those of their clients. Brokerage firms and stock brokers, on the other hand, have much different payment agreements. Their revenues may increase regardless of the performance of their customers' assets.

- Unlike brokerage firms, where investment banking and underwriting are commonplace, Registered Investment Advisors must manage money in the best interests of their customers. Because Registered Investment Advisors charge set fees for their services, their focus is on their client. Brokerage firms may focus on other aspects of the firm that do not contribute to the improvement of their clients' assets. Just to drive home the point, here is what a fiduciary duty to a client means for a Registered Investment Advisor. Registered Investment Advisors must:*

- Always act in the best interest of their client and make investment decisions that reflect their goals.

- Identify and monitor securities that are illiquid.

- When appropriate, employ fair market valuation procedures.

- Observe procedures regarding the allocation of investment opportunities, including new issues and the aggregation of orders.

- Have policies regarding affiliated broker-dealers and maintenance of brokerage accounts.

- Disclose all conflicts of interest.

- Have policies on use of brokerage commissions for research.

- Have policies regarding directed brokerage, including step-out trades and payment for order flow.

- Abide by a code of ethics.

CHAPTER 6 RECAP //

- When you take a loss on the stock market, you have to do more than just earn back your initial loss in order to get back to where you were before. The math of rebounds uses the percentage of the investment and not dollar amount to calculate what you need to earn in order to recapture your losses.
- The sequence of returns tells us that in addition to how the market performs, the order of those returns is just as important when it comes to calculating the value of our investments.
- Emotions inevitably enter the mix during stock market downturns. According to the DALBAR "Quantitative Analysis of Investment Behavior" report released in 2013, the average investor managing their money alone failed to keep up with inflation in nine out of the last 14 years.
- Financial professionals don't try to out-smart the market when managing investments for their clients. Instead, they tap into the potential for gains by committing to proven and long-term investment strategies.

7
WHAT IS YELLOW MONEY?

"Can anybody help me grow my money?"

Oscar is 69 years old. He retired four years ago. He relied on income from an IRA for three years in order to increase his Social Security benefit. He also made significant investments in 36 different mutual funds. He chose to diversify among the funds by selecting a portion for growth, another for good dividends, another that focused on promising small cap companies and a final portion that work like index funds. All the money that Oscar had in mutual funds he considered Need Later Money that he wanted to rely on in his 80s. After the stock market took a hit in 2008, Oscar lost some confidence in his investments and decided to sit down with a financial professional to see if his portfolio was able to recover.

The professional Oscar met with was able to determine what goals he had in mind. Specifically, the financial professional determined what Oscar actually wanted and needed the money for, and when he needed it. His professional also looked inside each of the mutual funds and discovered several instances of overlap. While Oscar had created diversity in his portfolio by selecting funds focused on different goals, he didn't account for overlap in the companies in which the funds were invested. Out of the 36 funds, his professional found that 20 owned nearly identical stock. While most of the companies were good investments, the high instance of overlap did not contribute to the healthy investment diversity that Oscar wanted. Oscar's financial professional also provided him with a report that explained the concentration ratio of his holdings (noting how much of his portfolio was contained within the top 25 stock holdings), the percentage of his portfolio that each company in which he invested in represented (showing the percentage of net assets that each company made up as an overall position in his portfolio) and the portfolio date of his account (showing when the funds in his portfolio were last updated: as funds are required to report updates only twice per year, it was possible that some of his fund reports could be six months old).

Oscar's professional consolidated his assets into one investment management strategy. This allowed Oscar's investments to be managed by someone he trusted who knew his specific investment goals and needs. Eliminating redundancy and overlap in his portfolio was easy to do but difficult to detect since Oscar had multiple funds with multiple brokerage firms. Oscar sat down with a professional to see if his mutual funds could perform well, and he left with a consolidated management plan and a money manager that understood him personally. That's Yellow Money at its best.

Now that you've calculated the Rule of 100, determined how much risk you have and how much you want, and you've determined how much Green Money you need to meet your short-term and mid-term income needs, it's time to look at what you have left. The money you have left after you've calculated your Green Money needs has the potential of becoming Red Money: your stocks, mutual funds and other investment products that you want to continue accumulating value with the market. You now have the luxury of taking a closer second look at your Red Money to determine how you would like to manage it.

As you read earlier in the key findings of the DALBAR report, the deck is stacked against the individual investor. Remember that the average investor on a fixed income failed to keep pace with inflation in nine of the last 14 years, meaning the inherent risk in managing your Red Money is very real and could have a lasting impact on your assets. So, how much of your Red Money do you invest, and in what kinds of markets, investment products and stocks do you invest? There are a lot of different directions in which you can take your Red Money. One thing is for sure: significant accumulation depends on investing in the market. How you go about doing it is different for everyone. Gathering stocks, bonds and investment funds together in a portfolio without a cohesive strategy behind them could cause you to miss out on the benefits of a more thoughtful and planful approach. The end result is that you may never really understand what your money is doing, where and how it is really invested, and which investment principles are behind the investment products you hold. While you may have goals for each individual piece of your portfolio, it is likely that you don't have a comprehensive plan for your Red Money, which may mean that *you are taking on more risk than you would like, and are getting less return for it than is possible.*

Enter **Yellow Money.** Yellow Money is money that is managed by a professional **with a purpose.** After your income needs are met and you have assets that you would like to dedicate to accumulation, there are decisions you need to make about how to invest those assets. You can buy stocks, index funds, mutual funds, bonds — you name it — you can invest in it. However, the difference between Red Money and Yellow Money is that Yellow Money has a cohesive strategy behind it that is *implemented by a professional*. When you manage your Red Money with an investment plan, it becomes Yellow Money: *money that is being managed with a specific purpose, a specific set of focused goals and a specific strategy in mind*. Yellow Money is still a type of Red Money. It comes with different levels of risk. But Yellow Money is under the watchful eye of professionals who have a stake in the success of your money in the market and who can recommend a range of strategies from those designed for preservation to those targeting rapid growth. You don't want to miss out on achieving the right level of risk, and more importantly, composing a careful plan for the return of your assets.

It can be helpful to think of Red Money and Yellow Money with this analogy:

If you needed to travel through an unfamiliar city in a foreign country, you could rent a car or perhaps hire a driver. Were you to drive yourself, you would try to gain guidance from perplexing road signs and need to adhere to traffic rules – with no experience or assistance to lean on. It would take longer to get to where you want to go, and the chance of a traffic accident would be higher. If you hired a driver, they would manage your journey. A driver would know the route, how to avoid traffic, and follow the rules of the road.

Red Money is like driving yourself. With Yellow Money, you are still traveling by car, but now you have a professional working on your behalf.

TAKING A CLOSER LOOK AT YOUR PORTFOLIO
Think about your investment portfolio. Think specifically of what you would consider your Red Money. Do you know what

is there? You may have several different investment products like individual mutual funds, bond accounts, stocks, and alternative investments. You may have inherited a stock portfolio from a relative, or you might be invested in a bond account offered by the company for which you worked due to your familiarity with them. While you may or may not be managing your investments individually, the reality is that you probably don't have an overall management strategy for all of your investments. Investments that aren't managed are simply Red Money, or money that is at risk in the market.

Harnessing the earning potential of your Red Money relies on more than a collection of stocks and bonds, however. It needs guided management. A good Yellow Money manager uses the knowledge they have about the level of risk with which you are comfortable, what you need or want to use your money for, when you want or need it and how you want to use it. The Yellow Money objects that they choose for you will still have a certain level of risk, but under the right management, control and process, you have a far better chance of a successful outcome that meets your specific needs.

When you sit down with an investment professional, you can look at all of your assets together. Chances are that you have accumulated a number of different assets over the last 20, 30 or 50 years. You may have a 401(k), an IRA, a Roth IRA, an account of self-directed stocks, a brokerage account, etc. Wherever you put your money, a financial professional will go through your assets and help you determine the level of risk to which you are exposed now and should be exposed in the future.

AVOIDING EMOTIONAL INVESTING

There's no way around it; people get emotional about their money. And for good reason. You've spent your life working for it, exchanging your time and talent for it, and making decisions about how to invest it, save it and make it grow. The maintenance of your lifestyle and your plans for retirement all depend on it. The best investment strategies, however, don't rely on emotions. One of Yellow Money's greatest strengths lies in the fact that it is managed by someone who understands your needs and desires, but doesn't make decisions about your money under the influence of emotion.

A well-managed investment account meets your goals as a whole, not in individualized and piecemeal ways. Professional money managers do this by creating requirements for each type of investment in which they put your money. We'll call them "screens." Your money manager will run your holdings through the screens they have created to evaluate different types of investment strategies. A professionally managed account will only have holdings that meet the requirements laid out in the overall management plan that was designed to meet your investment goals. The holdings that don't make it through the screens, the ones that don't contribute to your investment goals, are sold and redistributed to investments that your financial professional has determined to be appropriate.

Different screens apply to different Yellow Money strategies. For example, if one of your goals is significant growth, which would require taking on more risk alongside the potential for more return, an investment professional would screen for companies that have high rates of revenue and sales growth, high earnings growth, rising profit margins, and innovative products. On the other hand, if you want your portfolio to be used for income, which would call for lower risk and less return, your professional would screen for dividend yield and sector diversification. *Every investor has a different goal, and every goal requires a customized strategy that uses quantitative screens.* A professional will create a portfolio that reflects your investment desires. If some of the current assets you own complement the strategies that your professional recommends, those will likely stay in your portfolio.

Screening your assets removes emotions from the equation. It removes attachment to underperforming or overly risky investments. Financial professionals aren't married to particular stocks or mutual funds for any reason. They go by the numbers and see your portfolio through a lens shaped by your retirement goals. Your professional understands your wants and needs, and creates an investment strategy that takes your life events and future plans into account. It's a planful approach, and it allows you to tap into the tools and resources of a professional who has built a career around successful investing. Managing money is a full-time job and is best left to a professional money manager.

Removing emotions from investing also allows you to be unaffected by the day-to-day volatility of the market. Your financial professional doesn't ask where the market is going to be in a year, three years or a month from now. If you look at the value of the stock market from the beginning of the twentieth century to today, it's going up. Despite the Great Depression, despite the 1987 crash, despite the 2008 market downturn, the market, as a whole, trends up. Remember the major market downturn in 2008 when the market lost 30 percent of its value? Not only did it completely recover, it has far exceeded its 2008 value. Emotional investing led countless people to sell low as the market went down, and buy the same shares back when the market started to recover. That's an expensive way to do business. While you can't afford to lose money that you need in two, three or five years, your Need Later Money has time to grow. The best way to do so is to make it Yellow.

CREATING AN INVESTMENT STRATEGY

Chances are that you can benefit from taking a more managed investment approach tailored to your goals. Yellow Money is generally Need Later Money that you want to grow for needs you'll have in at least 10 years. You can work with your financial planner to create investments that meet your needs within different timeframes. You may need to rely on some of your Yellow Money in 10, 15 or 20 years, whether for additional income, a large purchase you plan on making or a vacation. Whatever you want it for, you will need it down the road. A financial professional can help you rescale the risk of your assets as they grow, helping you lock in your profits and secure a source of income you can depend on later.

So what does a Yellow Money account look like? Here's what it *doesn't* look like: a portfolio with 49 small cap mutual funds, a dozen individual stocks and an assortment of bond accounts. A brokerage account with a hodgepodge of investments, even if goal-oriented, is not a professionally managed account. It's still Red Money. Remember, Yellow Money is a managed account that has an overarching investment philosophy. When you look at making investments that will perform to meet your future income needs, the burning question becomes: How much should you have in the market and how should it be invested? Working with a professional will help you determine how much risk you should take, how to balance your assets so they will meet your goals and how to plan for the big ticket items, like health care expenses, that may be in your future. Yes, Yellow Money is exposed to risk, but by working with a professional, you can manage that risk in a productive way.

WHY YELLOW MONEY?

If you have met your immediate income needs for retirement, why bother with professionally managing your other assets? The money you have accumulated above and beyond your income needs probably has a greater purpose. It may be for your children or grandchildren. You may want to give money to a charity or organization that you admire. In short, you may want to craft your legacy. It would be advantageous to grow your assets in the best manner possible. A financial professional has built a career around managing money in profitable ways. They are experts under the supervision of the organization that they represent.

Turning to Yellow Money also means that you don't have to burden yourself with the time commitment, the stress, and the cost of determining how to manage your money. Yellow Money can help you better enjoy your retirement. Do you want to sit down in your home office every day and determine how to best allocate your assets, or do you want to be living your life while someone else manages your money for you? When the majority of your Red Money is managed with a specific purpose by a financial professional, you don't have to be worrying about which stocks to buy and sell today or tomorrow.

SEEKING FINANCIAL ADVICE: STOCK BROKERS VS. INVESTMENT ADVISOR REPRESENTATIVES

Investors basically have access to two types of advice in today's financial world: advice from stock brokers and advice given by investment advisors. Most investors, however, don't know the difference between types of advice and the people from whom they receive advice. Today, there are two primary types of advice offered to investors: advice given by a commission-based registered representative (brokers) and advice given by fee-based Investment Advisor Representatives. Unfortunately, many investors are not aware that a difference exists; nor have they been explained the distinction between the two types of advice. In a survey taken by TD Ameritrade, the top reasons investors choose to work with an independent registered investment advisor are:*

2011 Advisor Sentiment Study, commissioned by TD AMERITRADE. TD Ameritrade, Inc.

- Registered Investment Advisors are required, as fiduciaries, to offer advice that is in the best interest of clients
- More personalized service and competitive fee structure offered at a Registered Investment Advisor firm
- Dissatisfaction with full commission brokers

The truth is that there is a great deal of difference between stock brokers and investment advisor representatives. For starters, investment advisor representatives are obligated to act in an investor's best interests in all aspects of a financial relationship. Confusion continues to exist among investors struggling to find the best financial advice out there and the most credible sources of advice.

Here is some information to help clear up the confusion so you can find good advice from a professional you can trust:

- Investment advisor representatives have the fiduciary duty to act in a client's best interest at all times with every investment decision they make. Stock brokers and brokerage firms usually do not act as fiduciaries to their investors and are not obligated to make decisions that are entirely in the best interest of their customers. For example, if you decide you want to invest in precious metals, a stock broker would offer you a precious metals account from their firm. An Investment Advisor would find you a precious metals account that is the best fit for you based on the investment strategy of your portfolio.
- Investment advisors give their clients a Form ADV describing the methods that the professional uses to do business. An Investment Advisor also obtains client consent regarding any conflicts of interest that could exist with the business of the professional.
- Stock brokers and brokerage firms are not obligated to provide comparable types of disclosure to their customers.

- Whereas stock brokers and firms routinely earn large profits by trading as principal with customers, Investment Advisors cannot trade with clients as principal (except in very limited and specific circumstances).
- Investment Advisors charge a pre-negotiated fee with their clients in advance of any transactions. They cannot earn additional profits or commissions from their customers' investments without prior consent. Registered Investment Advisors are commonly paid an asset-based fee that aligns their interests with those of their clients. Brokerage firms and stock brokers, on the other hand, have much different payment agreements. Their revenues may increase regardless of the performance of their customers' assets.
- Unlike brokerage firms, where investment banking and underwriting are commonplace, Registered Investment Advisors must manage money in the best interests of their customers. Because Registered Investment Advisors charge set fees for their services, their focus is on their client. Brokerage firms may focus on other aspects of the firm that do not contribute to the improvement of their clients' assets.

Just to drive home the point, here is what a fiduciary duty to a client means for a Registered Investment Advisor. Registered Investment Advisors must:*

- Always act in the best interest of their client and make investment decisions that reflect their goals.
- Identify and monitor securities that are illiquid.
- When appropriate, employ fair market valuation procedures.

---

*2011 Advisor Sentiment Study, commissioned by TD AMERITRADE. TD Ameritrade, Inc.

- Observe procedures regarding the allocation of investment opportunities, including new issues and the aggregation of orders.
- Have policies regarding affiliated broker-dealers and maintenance of brokerage accounts.
- Disclose all conflicts of interest.
- Have policies on use of brokerage commissions for research.
- Have policies regarding directed brokerage, including step-out trades and payment for order flow.
- Abide by a code of ethics.

CHAPTER 7 RECAP //

- Yellow Money is money that is managed by a professional with a purpose. It is still considered a type of Red Money, but there is a dedicated direction, strategy and end-goal in mind, which makes it less dangerous.
- Red Money is like driving yourself in unfamiliar territory. With Yellow Money, you are still traveling by car, but now you have a professional driving on your behalf.
- Yellow Money is managed without emotions. A financial professional manages the yellow money using a specific criteria designed to fit into your overall financial plan so that it works the way you want it to.

8

THE WAKE-UP CALL:
How to Secure Funds for the Unexpected

"What if I need my money?"

Helen is an 85 year-old widow still living on her own in San Antonio. Last summer she stepped on a little pebble; her foot rolled out from under her and she fell and broke her hip. She also had a few other fractures and because of her osteoporosis, her doctor determined she was no longer able to live in her home. He recommended that she move to an assisted living community, and that sounded all right to Helen, except that she didn't have a long term care policy. She was living on her Social Security benefit and because of her limited savings, she didn't qualify for Medicaid. She did, however, have a son who lived nearby in the community.

Helen's son, Walter, came to the rescue wearing his red cape. As her only son, he felt obligated to help out mom. The nursing home facility that Walter's mom moved to cost $60,000 a year. Her savings were able to cover $10,000 of that annually. It fell to Walter to come up with the additional $50,000 a year for the next who-knows-how-long to take care of mom. The question was, as a retiree, where would he get these funds?

WHAT WILL IT COST YOU?

Most retirees fear losing money to the stock market, but you can lose just as much money to other circumstances such as family emergencies and health care. If your mom needs help and as her only child you have the money saved in an IRA, would you be able to say no? Most people find that they cannot. The problem is that taking money from an IRA could have all sorts of tax repercussions, not to mention the hole it could leave in your income planning. This is why planning for Need Later Money is crucial to the long term health of a good income plan.

Walter in our story above was retired but he had seen a financial professional to plan for both Need Now and Need Later income. With the professional's help, they were able to set aside money that accomplished three things: security, growth, and access to liquidity. Liquidity is an important part of an income plan because when family emergencies happen, you need access to your cash. In the case of Walter, his professional solved this problem by using a laddered annuity strategy. Each of three annuities was set up to mature in five, seven and ten years down the road. When you purchase an annuity, most products allow you to access up to ten percent of your money annually as needed for cash emergencies. Furthermore, when an annuity matures, the contract ends and you can take the cash out PLUS all your gains. This strategy allowed Walter to have access to large pools of cash when his mom needed help. He also triggered the income rider on one of his annuities to help offset the expense of taking care of mom.

This strategy took into consideration the three factors liquidity, safety and return. Here is why these three factors must be considered when making a long-term investment plan.

WHAT YOU NEED TO KNOW ABOUT LIQUIDITY, SAFETY AND RETURN

Earlier we discussed how today's investment options require advice that is relevant to today. Traditional, outdated investment strategies are not only ineffective; they can be harmful to the average investor. One of the most traditional ways of thinking about investing is the risk versus reward trade-off. It goes something like this:

Investment options that are considered safer carry less risk, but also offer the potential for less return. Riskier investment options carry the burden of volatility and a greater potential for loss, but they also offer a greater potential for large rewards. Most professionals move their clients back and forth along this range, shifting between investments that are safer and investments that are structured for growth. Essentially, the old rules of investing dictate that you can either choose relative safety *or* return, but you can't have both.

Updated investment strategies work with the flexibility of liquidity to remake the rules. Here is how:

There are three dimensions that are inherent in any investment: *Liquidity, Safety,* and *Return.* You can maximize any two of these dimensions at the expense of the third. If you choose Safety and Liquidity, this is like keeping your assets in a checking account or savings account. This option delivers a lot of Safety and Liquidity, but at the expense of any Return. On the other hand, if you choose Liquidity and Return, meaning you have the potential for great return and can still reclaim your money whenever you choose, you will likely be exposed to a very high level of risk.

Understanding Liquidity can help you break the old Risk versus Safety trade-off. By identifying assets from which you don't require Liquidity, you can place yourself in a position to potentially profit from relatively safe investments that provide a higher than average rate of return.

Choosing Safety and Return over Liquidity can have significant impacts on the accumulation of your assets. In Walter's case, by utilizing new investment tools and strategies, he was able to capitalize on the benefits of all three, liquidly, safety *and* return, which allowed him to swoop in and save the day when mom needed him.

TOOLS FOR A BLENDED APPROACH

Alternative investments can offer a way to really hit a home run, helping you to achieve growth, guarantee of principal and access to your funds should an emergency come up. Today's newer, fixed indexed annuities can offer a way to achieve liquidity, safety and return all in one product if you don't need to access the money all at once. A FIA without an income rider can be kept as a liquid account that you can access as needed for emergencies if it's not a key component in your lifetime income plan.

As in the case of Walter's mother, something as small and innocuous as a pebble really threw a wrench into the works. Using a combination of FIAs with income riders, Walter's financial professional was able to come up with a solution for his Need Later Money needs that didn't compromise the funds he was relying on for income. Other life insurance products that can work alone or in concert include the Indexed Universal Life insurance, or IUL. You can put money into an IUL in the same way you would put money into a Roth IRA, but without the set limits. An IUL allows you to make contributions at today's tax rate so that can pull it out later *without* being taxed. As with all investments products, annuities and IULs all have different risks involved and different rewards depending on your income and growth needs.

It's all about getting the right tool for the job. The sooner you want your money back, the less you can leverage it for Safety or Return. If you have the option of putting your money in a long-term investment, you will be sacrificing Liquidity, but potentially gaining both Safety and Return. Rethinking your approach to money in a way that includes the concepts of liquidity, safety and return can make a world of difference in the viability of your Need Later Money plan. Utilizing this strategy can provide you with a structured way to generate income while allowing the value of your asset to grow over time.

How much Liquidity do you **really** need? Think about it. If you haven't sat down and created an income plan for your retirement, your perceived need for Liquidity is a guess. You don't know how much cash you'll need to fill the income gap if you don't know the amount of your Social Security benefit or the total of your other income options. If you have determined your income needs and have made a plan for filling your income gap, you can now partition your assets based on when you will need them. An income plan that includes both Need Now and Need Later Money can use new rules, strategies and investment tools so you can enjoy both Safety and Return from your assets, *and* have access to the cash when you need it.

CHAPTER 8 RECAP //

- The three aspects of any investment include liquidity, safety, and return. You can choose to maximize any two against the third. Or you can use new investment tools designed for today's retirees and work with a financial professional to use a blended approach. With the right tools and strategies, it is possible to achieve all three aspects.
- Choosing to maximize liquidity alone can be an expensive option because the sooner you need your money back, the less you can leverage it for safety and return.
- To plan for a successful retirement in today's economy requires a creative use of today's financial tools.

9

THE TAX MAN AND
YOUR RETIREMENT

"Who is first in line?"

George and Leslie, a 62-year-old couple, begin working with a financial professional in October. After structuring their assets to reflect their risk tolerance and creating assets that would provide them Green Money income during retirement, they feel good about their situation. They make decisions that allow them to maximize their Social Security benefits, they have plenty of options for filling their income gap, and have begun a safe yet ambitious Yellow Money strategy with their professional. When their professional asks them about their tax plan, they tell him their CPA handled their taxes every year, and did a great job. Their professional says, "I don't mean who does your taxes, I mean, who does your tax planning?"

George and Leslie aren't sure how to respond.

Their professional brings George and Leslie's financial plan to the firm's CPA and has her run a tax projection for them. A week later their professional calls them with a tax plan for the year that will save them more than $3,000 on their tax return. The couple is shocked. A simple piece of advice from the CPA based on the numbers revealed that if they paid their estimated taxes before the end of the year, they would be able to itemize it as a deduction, allowing them to save thousands of dollars.

This solution won't work for everyone, and it may not work for George and Leslie every year. That's not the point. By being proactive with their approach to taxes and using the resources made available by their financial professional, they were able to create a tax plan that saved them money.

Tax planning and **tax reporting** are two very different things. Most people only *report* their taxes. March rolls around, people pull out their 1040s or use TurboTax to enter their income and taxable assets, and ship it off to Uncle Sam at the IRS. If you use a CPA to report your taxes, you are essentially paying them to record history. Doing your taxes in January, February, March or April means you are writing a history book. Planning your taxes in October, November or December means that you are writing the story as it happens. You can look at all the factors that are at play and make decisions that will impact your tax return *before* you file it.

You have the option of being proactive with your taxes and to plan for your future by making smart, informed decisions about how taxes affect your overall financial plan. When you retire, you move from the earning and accumulation phase of your life into the asset distribution phase of your life. For most people, that means relying on Social Security, a 401(k), an IRA, or a pension. Wherever you have put your Green Money for retirement, you are going to start relying on it to provide you with the income that once came as a paycheck. Most of these distributions will be considered income by the IRS and will be taxed as such. There are exceptions to that (not all of your Social Security income is taxed, and income from Roth IRAs is not taxed), but for the most part, your distributions will be subject to income taxes.

Working with a financial professional who, along with a CPA, makes recommendations about your finances to you, will keep you looking forward instead of in the rearview mirror as you enter retirement.

WHO IS FIRST IN LINE? THE TAX MAN AND YOUR RETIREMENT

When you retire, you move from the earning and accumulation phase of your life into the asset distribution phase of your life. For most people, that means relying on Social Security, a 401(k), an IRA, or a pension. Wherever you have put your Green Money for retirement, you are going to start relying on it to provide you with the income that once came as a paycheck. Most of these distributions will be considered income by the IRS and the Tax Man will be standing by, waiting for his share. There are exceptions to that (not all of your Social Security income is taxed, and income from Roth IRAs is not taxed), but for the most part, your distributions are considered income and the Tax Man will want his share.

Regarding assets that you have in an IRA or a 401(k) plan, when you reach 70 ½ years of age, you will be required to draw a certain amount of money from your IRA as income each year. That amount depends on your age and the balance in your IRA. The amount that you are required to withdraw as income is called a Required Minimum Distribution (RMD). Why are you required to withdraw money from your own account? Chances are the money in that account has grown over time, and the Tax Man wants to collect taxes on that growth. If you have a large balance in an IRA, there's a chance your RMD could increase your income significantly enough to put you into a higher tax bracket, subjecting you to a higher tax rate. This will make the Tax Man happy, but how will you feel about it?

Here's where tax planning can really begin to work strongly in your favor. In the distribution phase of your life, you have a predictable income based on your RMDs, your Social Security benefit and any other income-generating assets you may have. What really impacts you at this stage is how much of that money you keep in your pocket after taxes. Essentially, **you will make more money saving on taxes than you will by making more money.** If you can reduce your tax burden by 30, 20 or even 10 percent, you earn yourself that much more money by not paying it in taxes. In other words, the money goes into *your* wallet instead of into the hands of the Tax Man.

How do you save money on taxes? By having a plan. In this instance, a financial professional can work with the CPAs at their firm to create a distribution plan that minimizes your taxes and maximizes your annual net income.

BIG TAX MISTAKES AND HOW THEY IMPACT YOU

The average retirees are not looking to be multi-millionaires. They are looking to retire comfortably, and they don't have thousands or even hundreds of dollars they consider expendable. This is why money mistakes that can easily be avoided are so troubling. One of the biggest mistakes people make when planning for retirement on their own is failing to understand the tax ramifications of the money decisions they make. This section will clearly discuss the following common problem areas: Tax Ramifications on IRAs, Taxes and 401(k) Distributions, Tax Rules on Annuities, and The Estate Tax Dilemma.

The Tax Ramifications On IRAs: We touched on this subject earlier when discussing the risk aspects of investments that aren't understood. The thing to remember with a traditional IRA account is that if you don't set it up right, your beneficiaries will be paying your taxes. Most people think the money they inherit in an IRA is a tax-free gift. While it's true that gifts of money under a certain amount are not taxable, the money in your parent's IRA might have taxes due *because of where that money came from.* If that money came from your paycheck BEFORE the taxes were paid, then the taxes still have to be paid. The question is, over how many years will those tax payments be spread out?

The absolute latest you can start paying the Tax Man his share begins in the year after you reach that magic birthday of 70 ½. At that point, taxes begin to come due. The amount you owe in taxes is calculated by the Federal government based on average lifetime expectancy rates. So if you owe, for example, $70,000 in taxes on an IRA worth $350,000, that amount will be divided by the number of years they calculate that you have left to live. Should you leave this earth and pass that money on to your beneficiaries, you also pass onto them your tax debt. Not only do they have to pay the taxes on the money that you earned, but they have to pay it according to the federal guidelines of *your* life expectancy, and not theirs. That could mean your beneficiaries will have a five-year window to pay a $70,000 tax bill.

Proactive tax planning can help you avoid leaving this tax bomb for your beneficiaries. Your financial professional can help you go over your options.

401(k) Distribution: The thing to remember here is that money in a 401(k) is qualified money. What does this money qualify for? Taxes. You still owe taxes on this money. When you retire from your job, three things usually happen to the money in your 401(k) plan. First, your employer stops contributing money to the plan. That's not a surprise. You also stop contributing to the plan. However, your employer is still managing that money. Is that a good thing? Many 401(k) investment plans are designed for aggressive growth and aren't suitable vehicles for the lifetime savings of a new or soon-to-be retiree. Many senior citizens opt to roll this money over into an Individual Retirement Account such as an IRA. Doing that doesn't cause a tax issue. Yet.

Taxes become an issue the moment you start taking distributions on that money. Whether that time comes when you are 70 ½ or sooner, the taxes on that money have to be paid. In addition to those taxes, you have to be aware of what tax bracket the income from those distributions will throw you into. If you are also receiving Social Security and a pension, having to take an RMD in addition to paying those taxes could really amount to a huge tax burden.

Your financial professional can help design strategies for you to help alleviate the weight of this tax burden. The main strategy is what's known as a Roth Conversion. If you are still young – around age 55, for example – you can start moving that money directly from your 401(k) into a Roth IRA. Paying a portion on the taxes, we can invest the money into two or more annuities where it would grow tax-free for a period of five to seven years with the end game of paying the taxes gradually by spreading the tax liability out. After seven to 10 years, the money is converted into a Roth IRA and any withdrawals taken from the Roth IRA are totally tax free. AND you won't have any RMD because Roth IRAs don't come with a required minimum distribution. They don't have an RMD because the Tax Man isn't in line, waiting for his share. He's already been paid.

Not Understanding The Tax Rules On Distributions From Annuities: Most people understand that the gains earned by an annuity grow tax-deferred. But what happens when you need to tap into that annuity, such as the case with Walter, when he had to help pay the nursing home bill for his mom? Let's suppose you have $100,000 in an annuity and that money is non-qualified. (This means it doesn't qualify to be taxed. There is no Tax Man standing by because this was purchased with after tax money.) You put that money into an annuity contract, and it starts to earn interest and gains at an average rate of 5 percent per year. Those gains on that annuity are going to build on a tax-deferred basis. Each year that 5 percent is compounded.

Now, go down the road 10 years and that contract is worth $150,000. You think, great! Right? But remember, $50,000 of that money are gains, which means we have not paid the Tax Man yet. Say I want to take an income on that $150,000. What percent of my income will be taxed? 100 percent. That's right – 100 percent of any withdrawals you make that first year will be taxed because the Tax Man has a very important rule: Tax Man gets paid first. This is also what's known as last in, first out and it means the taxes on any gains are paid first before the principal is tapped. This is a process that usually takes about two to three years. Only the first $50,000 in this scenario will be taxed, and the rest is not, but this is something you need to be aware of when considering the need for liquidity. Another thing to remember is that if the account loses money and there are no gains, then there are no taxes on investments made with non-qualified money.

Not Understanding The Estate Tax Dilemma: Most people don't keep track of the current estate tax credit laws. It's not something they check every day like the weather or Facebook postings. But estate tax laws are changing every year. Ask your financial professional if a Life Insurance Trust might be a good strategy to employ if you are concerned about the tax liability owed by your heirs.

BUILDING A TAX DIVERSIFIED PORTFOLIO

So far so good: avoid taxes, maximize your net annual income and have a plan for doing it. When people decide to leverage the experience and resources of a financial professional, they may not be thinking of how distribution planning and tax planning will benefit their portfolios. Often more exciting prospects like planning income annuities, investing in the market and structuring investments for growth rule the day. Taxes, however, play a crucial role in retirement planning. Achieving those tax goals requires knowledge of options, foresight and professional guidance.

Finding the path to a good tax plan isn't always a simple task. Every tax return you file is different from the one before it because things constantly change. Your expenses change. Planned or unplanned purchases occur. Health care costs, medical bills, an inheritance, property purchases, reaching an age where your RMD kicks in or travel, any number of things can affect how much income you report and how many deductions you take each year.

Preparing for the ever-changing landscape of your financial life requires a tax-diversified portfolio that can be leveraged to balance the incomes, expenditures and deductions that affect you each year. A financial professional will work with you to answer questions like these:

- What does your tax landscape look like?
- Do you have a tax-diversified portfolio robust enough to adapt to your needs?
- Do you have a diversity of taxable and non-taxable income planned for your retirement?
- Will you be able to maximize your distributions to take advantage of your deductions when you retire?
- Is your portfolio strong enough and tax-diversified enough to adapt to an ever-changing (and usually increasing) tax code?

» *When Rae returns home after a week in the hospital recovering from a knee replacement, the 77-year-old calls her daughter, sister and brother to let them know she is home and feeling well. She also should have called her CPA. Rae's medical expenses for the procedure, her hospital stay, her medications and the ongoing physical therapy she attended amount to more than $50,000.*

Currently, Americans can deduct medical expenses that are more than 7.5 percent of their Adjusted Gross Income (AGI). Rae's AGI is $60,000 the year of her knee replacement, meaning she is able to deduct $44,000 of her medical bills from her taxes that year. Her AGI dictated that she could deduct more than 80 percent of her medical expenses that year. Rae didn't know this.

Had she been working with a financial professional who regularly asked her about any changes in her life, her spending, or her expenses (expected or unexpected), Rae could have saved thousands of dollars. Rae can also file an amendment to her tax return to recoup the overpayment.

This relatively simple example of how tax planning can save you money is just the tip of the iceberg. No one can be expected to know the entire U.S. tax code. But a professional who is working with a team of CPAs and financial professionals have an advantage over the average taxpayer who must start from square one on their own every year. Have you been taking advantage of all the deductions that are available to you?

PROACTIVE TAX PLANNING

The implications of proactive tax planning are far reaching, and are larger than many people realize. Remember, doing your taxes in January, February, March or April means you are writing a history book. Planning your taxes in October, November or December means that you are writing the story as it happens. You can look at all the factors that are at play and make decisions that will impact your tax return *before* you file it.

Realizing that tax planning is an aspect of financial planning is an important leap to make. When you incorporate tax planning into your financial planning strategy, it becomes part of the way you maximize your financial potential. Paying less in taxes means you keep more of your money. Simply put, the more money you keep, the more of it you can leverage as an asset. This kind of planning can affect you at any stage of your life. If you are 40 years old, are you contributing the maximum amount to your 401(k) plan? Are you contributing to a Roth IRA? Are you finding ways to structure the savings you are dedicating to your children's education? Do you have life insurance? Taxes and tax planning affects all of these investment tools. Having a relationship with a professional who works with a CPA can help you build a truly comprehensive financial plan that not only works with your investments, but also shapes your assets to find the most efficient ways to prepare for tax time. There may be years that you could benefit from higher distributions because of the tax bracket that you are in, or there could be years you would benefit from taking less. There may be years when you have a lot of deductions and years you have relatively few. Adapting your distributions to work in concert with your available deductions is at the heart of smart tax planning. Professional guidance can bring you to the next level of income distribution, allowing you to remain flexible enough to maximize your tax efficiency. And remember, saving money on taxes makes you more money than making money does.

What you have on paper is important: your assets, savings, investments, which are financial expression of your work and time. It's just as important to know how to get it off the paper in a way that keeps most of it in your pocket. Almost anything that involves financial planning also involves taxes. Annuities, investments, IRAs, 401(k)s, 403(b), and many other investment options will have tax implications. Life also has a way of throwing curveballs. Illness, expensive car repair or replacement, or any event that has a financial impact on your life will likely have a corresponding tax implication around which you should adapt your financial plan. Tax planning does just that.

One dollar can end up being less than 25 cents to your heirs.

> » When Anthony's father passed away, he discovered that he was the beneficiary of his father's $500,000 IRA. Anthony has a wife and a family of four children, and he knew that his father had intended for a large portion of the IRA to go toward funding their college educations.
>
> After Anthony's father's estate is distributed, Anthony, who is 50 years old and whose two oldest sons are entering college, liquidates the IRA. By doing so, his taxable income for that year puts him in a 39.6 percent tax bracket, immediately reducing the value of the asset to $302,000. An additional 3.8 percent surtax on net investment income further diminishes the funds to $283,000. Liquidating the IRA in effect subjects much of Anthony's regular income to the surtax, as well. At this point, Anthony will be taxed at 43.4 percent.
>
> Anthony's state taxes are an additional 9 percent. Moreover, estate taxes on Anthony's father's assets claim another 22 percent. By the time the IRS is through, Anthony's income from the IRA will be taxed at 75 percent, leaving him with $125,000 of the original $500,000. While it would help contribute to the education of his children, it wouldn't come anywhere near completely paying for it, something the $500,000 could have easily done.

As the above example makes clear, leaving an asset to your beneficiaries can be more complicated than it may seem. In the case of a traditional IRA, after federal, estate and state taxes, the asset could literally diminish to as little as 25 percent of its value.

How does working with a professional help you make smarter tax decisions with your own finances? Any financial professional worth their salt will be working with a firm that has a team of trained tax professionals, including CPAs, who have an intimate knowledge of the tax code and how to adapt a financial plan to it.

YELLOW MONEY AND TAXES

There are also tax implications for the money that you have managed professionally. People with portions of their investment portfolio that are actively traded can particularly benefit from having a proactive tax strategy. Without going into too much detail, for tax purposes there are two kinds of investment money: qualified and non-qualified. Different investment strategies can have different effects on how you are taxed on your investments and the growth of your investments. Some are more beneficial for one kind of investment strategy over another. Determining how to plan for the taxation of non-qualified and qualified investments is fodder for holiday party discussions at accounting firms. While it may not be a stimulating topic for the average investor, you don't have to understand exactly how it works in order to benefit from it.

While there are many differences between qualified and non-qualified investments, the main difference is this: qualified plans are designed to give investors tax benefits by deferring taxation of their growth until they are withdrawn. Non-qualified investments are not eligible for these deferral benefits. As such, non-qualified investments are taxed whenever income is realized from them in the form of growth.

Actively and non-actively traded investments provide a simple example of how to position your investments for the best tax advantage. In an actively traded and managed portfolio, there is a high amount of buying and selling of stocks, bonds, funds,

ETFs, etc. If that active portfolio of non-qualified investments does well and makes a 20 percent return one year and you are in the 39.6 percent tax bracket, your net gain from that portfolio is only about 12 percent (39.6 percent tax of the 20 percent gain is roughly 8 percent.) In a passive trading strategy, you can use a qualified investment tool, such as an IRA, to achieve 13, 14 or 15 percent growth (much lower than the actively traded portfolio), but still realize a higher net return because the growth of the qualified investment is not taxed until it is withdrawn.

Does this mean that you have to always rely on a buy and hold strategy in qualified investment tools? Not necessarily. The question is, if you have qualified and non-qualified investments, where do you want to position your actively traded and managed assets? Incorporating a planful approach to positioning your investments for more beneficial taxation can be done many ways, but let's consider one example. Keeping your actively managed investment strategies inside an IRA or some other qualified plan could allow you to realize the higher gains of those investments without paying tax on their growth every year. Your more passively managed funds could then be kept in taxable, non-qualified vehicles and methods, and because you aren't realizing income from them on an annual basis by frequently trading them, they grow sheltered from taxation.

If you are interested in taking advantage of tax strategies that maximize your net income, you need the attentive strategies, experience and knowledge of a professional who can give you options that position you for profit. At the end of the day, what's important to you as the consumer is how much you keep, your after-tax take home.

ESTATE TAXES

The government doesn't just tax your income from investments while you're alive. They will also dip into your legacy.

While estate taxes aren't as hot of a topic as they were a few years ago, they are still an issue of concern for many people with assets. While taxes may not apply on estates that are less than $5 million, certain states have estate taxes with much lower exclusion ratios. Some are as low as $600,000. Many people may have to pay a state estate tax. One strategy for avoiding those types of taxes is to move assets outside of your estate. That can include gifting them to family or friends, or putting them into an irrevocable trust. Life insurance is another option for protecting your legacy.

CHAPTER 9 RECAP //

- When you report your taxes, you are paying to record history. When you *plan* your taxes with a financial professional, you are proactively finding the best options for your tax return. Planning proactively means more money in your wallet and less money into the hands of the Tax Man.

- It's important to understand the tax repercussions when tapping into assets from a 401(k) or a traditional IRA for use an income source. Money that is considered qualified by the Federal government must be taxed upon distribution. Any gains made on annuities will also be taxed even if the annuity was purchased with non-qualified money, and the Tax Man will want his money on the front end.

- At the age of 70 ½, the Federal Government requires all IRA participants to begin taking their annual RMDs, or Required Minimum Distributions. Failure to take your RMD in a timely manner can cost you thousands of dollars in taxes and penalty fees.

- Taxes play an important role during your retirement. It's important that you understand your obligations, and the differences between tax-deferred and tax-advantaged accounts.

- You make more money by saving on taxes than you do by making more money. This simple concept becomes extremely valuable to people in retirement and those living on fixed incomes.

10

THE BRANDEIS STORY

"Should I convert my IRA?"

Louis Brandeis provides one of the best examples illustrating how tax planning works. Brandeis was Associate Justice on the Supreme Court of the United States from 1916 to 1939. Born in Louisville, Kentucky, Brandeis was an intelligent man with a touch of country charm. He described tax planning this way:

"I live in Alexandria, Virginia. Near the Court Chambers, there is a toll bridge across the Potomac. When in a rush, I pay the dollar toll and get home early. However, I usually drive outside the downtown section of the city and cross the Potomac on a free bridge.

The bridge was placed outside the downtown Washington, D.C. area to serve a useful social service – getting drivers to drive the extra mile and help alleviate congestion during the rush hour.

If I went over the toll bridge and through the barrier without paying a toll, I would be committing tax evasion.

If I drive the extra mile and drive outside the city of Washington to the free bridge, I am using a legitimate, logical and suitable method of tax avoidance, and I am performing a useful social service by doing so.

The tragedy is that few people know that the free bridge exists. *"*

Like Brandeis, most American taxpayers have options when it comes to "crossing the Potomac," so to speak. It's a financial planner's job to tell you what options are available. You can wait until March to file your taxes, at which time you might pay someone to report and pay the government a larger portion of your income. However, you could instead file before the end of the year, work with your financial professional and incorporate a tax plan as part of your overall financial planning strategy. Filing later is like crossing the toll bridge. Tax planning is like crossing the free bridge.

Which would you rather do?

The answer to this question is easy. Most people want to save money and pay less in taxes. What makes this situation really difficult in real life, however, is that the signs along the side of the road that direct us to the free bridge are not that clear. To normal Americans, and to plenty of people who have studied it, the U.S. tax code is easy to get lost in. There are all kinds of rules, exceptions to rules, caveats and conditions that are difficult to understand, or even to know about. What you really need to know is your options and the bottom line impacts of those options.

ROTH IRA CONVERSIONS

The attractive qualities of Roth IRAs may have prompted you to explore the possibility of moving some of your assets into a Roth account. Another important difference between the accounts is how they treat Required Minimum Distributions (RMDs). When you turn 70 ½ years old, you are required to take a minimum amount of money out of a traditional IRA. This amount is your RMD. It is treated as taxable income. Roth IRAs, however, do not have RMDs, and their distributions are not taxable. Quite a deal, right?

While having a Roth IRA as part of your portfolio is a good idea, converting assets to a Roth IRA can pose some challenges, depending on what kinds of assets you want to transfer.

One common option is the conversion of a traditional IRA to a Roth IRA. You may have heard about converting your IRA to a Roth IRA, but you might not know the full net result on your income. The main difference between the two accounts is that the growth of investments within a traditional IRA is not taxed until income is withdrawn from the account, whereas taxes are charged on contribution amounts to a Roth IRA, not withdrawals. The problem, however, is that when assets are removed from a traditional IRA, even if the assets are being transferred to a Roth IRA account, taxes apply.

There are a lot of reasons to look at Roth conversions. People have a lot of money in IRAs, up to multiple millions of dollars. Even with $500,000, when they turn 70 ½ years old, their RMD is going to be approximately $18,000, and they have to take that out whether they want to or not. It's a tax issue. Essentially, if you will be subject to high RMDs, it could have impacts on how much of your Social Security is taxable, and on your tax bracket.

By paying taxes now instead of later on assets in a Roth IRA, you can realize tax-advantaged growth. You pay once and you're done paying. Your heirs are done paying. It's a powerful tool. Here's a simple example to show you how powerful it can be:

Imagine that you pay to convert a traditional IRA to a Roth. You have decided that you want to put the money in a vehicle that gives you a tax-advantaged income option down the road. If you pay a

25 percent tax on that conversion and the Roth IRA then doubles in value over the next 10 years, you could look at your situation as only having paid 12.5 percent tax.

The prospect of tax-advantaged income is a tempting one. While you have to pay a conversion tax to transfer your assets, you also have turned taxable income into tax free retirement money that you can let grow as long as you want without being required to withdraw it.

There are options, however, that address this problem. Much like the Brandeis story, there may be a "free bridge" option for many investors.

Your financial professional will likely tell you that it is not a matter of whether or not you should perform a Roth IRA conversion, it is a matter of how much you should convert and when.

Here are some of the things to consider before converting to a Roth IRA:

- If you make a conversion before you retire, you may end up paying higher taxes on the conversion because it is likely that you are in some of your highest earning years, placing you in the highest tax bracket of your life. It is possible that a better strategy would be to wait until after you retire, a time when you may have less taxable income, which would place you in a lower tax bracket.

- Many people opt to reduce their work hours from full-time to part-time in the years before they retire. If you have pursued this option, your income will likely be lower, in turn lowering your tax rate.

- The first years that you draw Social Security benefits can also be years of lower reported income, making it another good time frame in which to convert to a Roth IRA.

One key strategy to handling a Roth IRA conversion is to always be able to pay the cost of the tax conversion with outside money.

Structuring your tax year to include something like a significant deduction can help you offset the conversion tax. This way you aren't forced to take the money you need for taxes from the value of the IRA. The reason taxes apply to this maneuver is because when you withdraw money from a traditional IRA, it is treated as taxable income by the IRS. Your financial professional, with the help of the CPAs at their firm, may be able to provide you with options like after-tax money, itemized deductions or other situations that can pose effective tax avoidance options.

Some examples of avoiding Roth IRA conversions taxes include:

- *Using medical expenses that are above 10 percent of your Adjusted Gross Income.* If you have health care costs that you can list as itemized deductions, you can convert an amount of income from a traditional IRA to a Roth IRA that is offset by the deductible amount. Essentially, deductible medical expenses negate the taxes resulting from recording the conversion.

- *Individuals, usually small business owners, who are dealing with a Net Operating Loss (NOL).* If you have NOLs, but aren't able to utilize all of them on your tax return, you can carry them forward to offset the taxable income from the taxes on income you convert to a Roth IRA.

- *Charitable giving.* If you are charitably inclined, you can use the amount of your donations to reduce the amount of taxable income you have during that year. By matching the amount you convert to a Roth IRA to the amount your taxable income was reduced by charitable giving, you can essentially avoid taxation on the conversion. You may decide to double your donations to a charity in one year, giving them two years' worth of donations in order to offset the Roth IRA conversion tax on this year's tax return.

- *Investments that are subject to depletion.* Certain investments can kick off depletion expenses. If you make an investment and are subject to depletion expenses, they can be deducted and used to offset a Roth IRA conversion tax.

Not all of the above scenarios work for everyone, and there are many other options for offsetting conversion taxes. The point is that you have options, and your financial professional and tax professional can help you understand those options.

If you have a traditional IRA, Roth conversions are something you should look at. As you approach retirement you should consider your options and make choices that keep more of your money in your pocket, not the government's.

ADDITIONAL TAX BENEFITS OF ROTH IRAS

Not only do Roth IRAs provide you with tax-advantaged growth, they also give you a tax diversified landscape that allows you to maximize your distributions. Chances are that no matter the circumstances, you will have taxed income and other assets subject to taxation. But if you have a Roth IRA, you have the unique ability to manage your Adjusted Gross Income (AGI), because you have a tax-advantaged income option!

Converting to a Roth IRA can also help you preserve and build your legacy. Because Roth IRAs are exempt from RMDs, after you make a conversion from a traditional IRA, your Roth account can grow tax-advantaged for another 15, 20 or 25 years and it can be used as tax-advantaged income by your heirs. It is important to note, however, that non-spousal beneficiaries do have to take RMDs from a Roth IRA, or choose to stretch it and draw tax-advantaged income out of it over their lifetime.

TO CONVERT OR NOT TO CONVERT?

Conversions aren't only for retirees. You can convert at any time. Your choice should be based on your individual circumstances and tax situation. Sticking with a traditional IRA or converting to a Roth, again, depends on your individual circumstances, including your income, your tax bracket and the amount of deductions you have each year.

Is it better to have a Roth IRA or traditional IRA? It depends on your individual circumstance. Some people don't mind having taxable income from an IRA. Their income might not be very high and their RMD might not bump their tax bracket up, so it's not as big a deal. A similar situation might involve income from Social Security. Social Security benefits are taxed based on other income you are drawing. If you are in a position where none or very little of your Social Security benefit is subject to taxes, paying income tax on your RMD may be very easy.

> » *There are also situations where leveraging taxable income from a traditional IRA can work to your advantage come tax time. For example, Darrel and Linda dream of buying a boat when they retire. It is something they have looked forward to their entire marriage. In addition to the savings and investments that they created to supply them with income during retirement, which includes a traditional IRA, they have also saved money for the sole purpose of purchasing a boat once they stop working.*
>
> *When the time comes and they finally buy the boat of their dreams, they pay an additional $15,000 in sales taxes that year because of the large purchase. Because they are retired and earning less money, the deductions they used to be able to realize from their income taxes are no longer there. The high amount of sales taxes they paid on the boat puts them in a*

position where they could benefit from taking taxable income from a traditional IRA..

When Darrel and Linda's financial professional learns about their purchase, he immediately contacts a CPA at his firm to run the numbers. They determine that by taking a $15,000 distribution from their IRA, they could fulfill their income needs to offset the $15,000 sales tax deduction that they were claiming due to the purchase of their boat. In the end, they pay zero taxes on their income distribution from their IRA.

The moral of the story? Having a tax diversified landscape gives you options. Having capital assets that can be liquidated, tax-advantaged income options and sources that can create capital gains or capital losses will put you in a position to play your cards right no matter what you want to accomplish with your taxes. The ace up your sleeve is your financial professional and the CPAs they work with. Do yourself a favor and *plan* your taxes instead of *reporting* them!

CHAPTER 10 RECAP //

- Look for the "free bridge" option in your tax strategy.
- Converting from a traditional to a Roth IRA can provide you with tax-advantaged retirement income.
- Converting to a Roth IRA can also help you preserve and build your legacy.
- There are many ways to reduce your taxes. Being smart about your Roth IRA conversion is one of the main ways to do so.

11
THE FUTURE OF U.S. TAXATION

"When will my taxes go up?"

If you were one of the people who raised your hand in response to the question, "How many people think taxes will go up?" a brief look at American history will further prove you right. The process of raising taxes takes several years to go from planning to implementation. Understanding why this is so and gaining insight into the process can help you make better choices when considering tax-advantaged options for your retirement savings.

DEBT CEILING – CAUSE AND EFFECTS
The raising of the debt ceiling raised more than just the ability for our government to go further into debt. It also raised concerns

and fears about the future of our economy. We are now seeing major swings in the markets with investors showing serious concerns over the future of investment valuations and their personal wealth. Unfortunately, the reasoning behind all of this uncertainty is preceded by the inability to see the full implications of what is in store. We rarely talk about the fact that the discussions on raising the debt ceiling were coupled to discussions on major tax reforms needed to correct the problems underlining the debt ceiling increase itself.

Increasing the debt ceiling was needed because the government maxed out its credit card, so to speak, which it has been living off of for quite some time. It is really not much different than what we have been seeing from the general public for the past few decades. Unfortunately, most of us do not have the ability to get a credit limit increase on our credit cards once we reach the maximum limit, that is unless we can show the ability to pay this balance back. The only way to pay this credit card back is by spending less and making more money.

This is exactly where the federal government is today. They have been given a higher credit limit, but they still must find a way to decrease the spending while making more money. The only way the government makes money is by collecting taxes.

Unfortunately, at the current moment, the government is collecting approximately $120 billion less per month than it currently spends. Discussions for major tax reform have accompanied the discussions for the increased debt ceiling.

DEBT AND EARNINGS
Let us take a closer look at where we are today. The U.S. national debt is increasing at an alarming rate, rising to levels never seen before and threatening serious harm to the economy. Through the end of 2010, the national debt has risen to $13.6 trillion, averaging an 11.4 percent increase annually over the past five years and

a 9.2 percent increase annually over the past 10 years. To put this into perspective, the national gross domestic product (GDP) has increased to $14.5 trillion during the same period, averaging a 2.9 percent annual increase over the past five years and a 3.9 percent increase over the past 10 years. At the end of 2010, the national debt level was 93 percent of the GDP. Economists believe that a sustainable economy exists at a maximum level of approximately 80 percent. As of December 20, 2013, the U.S. national debt is 107.69 percent of GDP with the debt at $17.252 trillion and the GDP at $16.020 trillion.*

The significance of these two numbers lies within the contrast. The national debt is the amount that needs to be repaid. This is the credit card balance. Gross domestic product on the other hand is less known and represents the market value of all final goods and services produced within a country during a given period. Essentially, GDP represents the gross taxable income available to the government. If debts are increasing at a greater rate than the gross income available for taxation, then the only way to make up the difference is by increasing the rate at which the gross income is taxed.

The most recent presidential budget shows a continuing trend in the disparity between growth in the national debt and GDP over the next two decades. Although the increasing disparity is a real concern and shows that, at least in the short run, the federal deficit will not be addressed to counteract the potential crisis ahead, it is the revenue collection that tells the disconcerting story. Over the past 40 years the average collection of GDP has been approximately 17.6 percent and currently collections are at approximately 14.4 percent of GDP.

As the presidential budget reveals, the projected revenues are estimated to be 20 percent by the end of the next decade. That

---

*http://www.usdebtclock.org/12/20/13

is a 38.8 percent increase from the current tax levels. To put this into perspective, if you are currently in the top tax bracket of 35 percent and this bracket increases by the proposed collection increase, your tax rate will be approximately 48.5 percent. Keep in mind that even at this rate the deficit is projected to increase.

2013 – THE END OF AN ERA?

From a historical point of view, taxes are extremely low. The last time the U.S. national debt was at the same percentage level of GDP as today was at the end of World War II and several years following. The maximum tax rate averaged 90 percent from 1944 through 1963. Compare that to the maximum rate of 35 percent today and it becomes very clear that there is a disparity of extreme proportion.

Taxes during this historical period were at extreme levels for nearly 20 years, during and following this current level of debt-to-GDP. A significant point to note about the difference between that time and today is the economic activity. The period of 1944 through 1963 was in the heart of both the industrial revolution and the birth of the Baby Boom generation. Today, we are mired in extreme volatility with frequent periods of boom and bust at the same time we are witnessing the beginning of the greatest retirement wave ever experienced within the U.S. economy.

To contrast these two time periods in respect to the recovery period is almost asinine as the external pressures from globalization and domestic unfunded liabilities did not exist or were irrelevant factors during the prior period.

To add insult to injury, U.S. domestic unfunded liabilities are currently estimated somewhere around $61.6 trillion due to items such as Social Security, Medicare and government pensions. The most concerning part of this pertains to the coming wave of retirement as the Baby Boom generation begins retiring and drawing on the unfunded Social Security for which they currently have entitlement. Over the long run, expenditures related to healthcare programs such as Medicare and Medicaid are projected to grow faster than the economy overall as the population matures.

To put unfunded liabilities into perspective, consider these as off-balance-sheet obligations similar to those of Enron. Although these are not listed as part of the national debt, they must be paid. These liabilities exist outside of the annual budgetary debt discussed. The difference between Enron and the U.S. unfunded liabilities is that if the U.S. government cannot come up with the funds to pay all these liabilities through revenue generation, they will print the money necessary to pay the debt.

WHAT DOES THE SOLUTION LOOK LIKE?

Unfortunately, the general public is in a no-win situation for this solution to the problem. Printing money does not bode well for economic growth. This creates inflationary pressures that devalue the U.S. dollar and make everyone less wealthy. Cutting the entitlements that compose this liability leaves millions of people without benefits they have come to expect. The only other option, and one that the government knows all too well, is increasing taxes. In fact, according to a Congressional Budget Office paper issued in 2004:

"The term 'unfunded liability' has been used to refer to a gap between the government's projected financial commitment under a particular program and the revenues that are expected to be available to fund that commitment. But no government obligation can be truly considered 'unfunded' because of the U.S. government's sovereign power to tax – which is the ultimate resource to meet its obligations."

A balanced budget will be required at some point and with this will come higher taxes. We have uncertainty surrounding tax rates and how high they will go. At that time, extensions put in place in December 2010 on Bush-era tax cuts are set to expire. We are likely to see some tax increases at this point. Whether it is only on the top earners or unilaterally across all income levels is yet to be seen, but an increase of some sort will most certainly occur.

How do you prepare? Why spend so much time reassuring you that taxes will increase? Because you have an opportunity to take action. Now is the time to prepare for what will come and structure countermeasures for the good, the bad and the ugly of each of these legislative nightmares through tax-advantaged retirement planning.

You make more money by saving on taxes than you do by making more money. The simplistic logic of the statement makes sense when you discover it takes $1.50 in earnings to put that same dollar, saved in taxes, back in your pocket.

As simple as it sounds, it is much more difficult to execute. Most people fail to put together a plan as they near retirement, beginning with a simple cash flow budget. If you have not analyzed your proposed income streams and expenses, you could not possibly have taken the time to position these cash flows and other events into a tax-preferred plan.

Most people will state that they have a plan and, thus, do not need any further assistance in this area. The truth in most instances is that people could not show you their plan, and among the few that could, most would not be able to show you how they have executed it. In this regard, they might as well be Richard Nixon stating, "I am not a crook" for as much as they state, "I have a plan." The truth lies in waiting. As we approach or begin retirement, we should look at what cash flows we will have. Do we have a pension? How about Social Security? How much additional cash flow am I going to need to draw from my assets to maintain the lifestyle that I desire?

We spend our whole lives saving and accumulating wealth but spend so little time determining how to distribute this accumulation so as to retain it. We need to make sure we have the appropriate diversification of taxable versus non-taxable assets to complement our distribution strategy.

THE BENEFITS OF DIVERSIFICATION

Heading into retirement, we should be situated with a diversified tax landscape. The point to spending our whole lives accumulating wealth is not to see the size of the number on paper, but rather to be an exercise in how much we put in our pocket after removing it from the paper. To truly understand tax diversification, we must understand what types of money exist and how each of these will be treated during accumulation and, most importantly, during distribution. The following is a brief summary:

1. Free money
2. Tax-advantaged money
3. Tax-deferred money
4. Taxable money
   a. Ordinary income
   b. Capital gains and qualified dividends

FREE MONEY

Free money is the best kind of money regardless of tax treatment because, in the end, you have more money than you would have otherwise. Many employers will provide contributions toward employee retirement accounts to offer additional employment benefits and encourage employees to save for their own retirement. With this, employers often will offer a matching contribution in which they contribute up to a certain percentage of an employee's salary (generally three to five percent) toward that employee's retirement account when the employee contributes to their retirement account as well. For example, if an employee earns $50,000 annually and contributes three percent ($1,500) to their retirement account annually, the employer will also contribute three percent ($1,500) to the employee's account. That is

$1,500 in free money. Take all you can get! Bear in mind that any employer contribution to a 401(k) will still be subject to taxation when withdrawn.

TAX-ADVANTAGED MONEY

Tax-advantaged money is the next best thing to free money. Although you have to earn tax-advantaged money, you do not have to give part of it away to Uncle Sam. Tax-advantaged money comes in three basic forms that you can utilize during your lifetime; four if prison inspires your future, but we are not going to discuss that option.

One of the most commonly known forms of tax-advantaged money is municipal bonds, which earn and pay interest that could be tax-advantaged on the federal level, or state level, or both. There are several caveats that should be discussed with regard to the notion of tax-advantaged income from municipal bonds. First, you will notice that tax-advantaged has several flavors from the state and federal perspective. This is because states will generally tax the interest earned on a municipal bond unless the bond is offered from an entity located within that state. This severely limits the availability of completely tax-advantaged municipal bonds and constrains underlying risk and liquidity factors. Second, municipal bond interest is added back into the equation for determining your modified adjusted gross income (MAGI) for Social Security. This could push your income above a threshold and subject a portion of your Social Security income to taxation.

In effect, if this interest subjects some other income to taxation then this interest is truly being taxed.

Last, municipal bond interest may be excluded from the regular federal tax system, but it is included for determining tax under the alternative minimum tax (AMT) system. In its basic form, the AMT system is a separate tax system that applies if the tax computed under AMT exceeds the tax computed under the regular tax system. The difference between these two computations is the alternative minimum tax.

TAX-ADVANTAGED MONEY: ROTH IRA

Roth accounts are probably the single greatest tax asset that has come from Congress outside of life insurance. They are well known but rarely used. Roth IRAs were first established by the Taxpayer Relief Act of 1997 and named after Senator William Roth, the chief sponsor of the legislation. Roth accounts are simply an account in the form of an individual retirement account or an employer sponsored retirement account that allows for tax-advantaged growth of earnings and, thus, tax-advantaged income.

The main difference between a Roth and a traditional IRA or employer-sponsored plan lies in the timing of the taxation. We are all very familiar with the typical scenario of putting money away for retirement through an employer plan, whereby they deduct money from our paychecks and put it directly into a retirement account. This money is taken out before taxes are calculated, meaning we do not pay tax on those earnings today. A Roth account, on the other hand, takes the money after the taxes have been removed and puts it into the retirement account, so we do pay tax on the money today. The other significant difference between these two is taxation during distribution in later years. Regarding our traditional retirement accounts, when we take the money out later it is added to our ordinary income and is taxed accordingly. Additionally, including this in our income subjects us to the consequences mentioned above for municipal bonds with Social Security taxation, AMT, as well as higher Medicare premiums. A Roth on the other hand is distributed tax-advantaged and does not contribute toward negative impact items such as Social Security taxation, AMT, or Medicare premium increases. It essentially comes back to us without tax and other obligations.

The best way to view the difference between the two accounts is to look at the life of a farmer. A farmer will buy seed, plant it in the ground, grow the crops and harvest it later for sale. Typically, the farmer would only pay tax on the crops that have been harvested and sold. But if you were the farmer, would you rather pay tax on the $5,000 of seed that you plant today or the $50,000 of crops harvested later? The obvious answer is $5,000 of seed today. The truth to the matter is that you are a farmer, except you plant dollars into your retirement account instead of seeds into the earth.

So why doesn't everyone have a Roth retirement account if things are so simple? There are several reasons, but the single greatest reason has been the constraints on contributions. If you earned over certain thresholds (MAGI over $125,000 single and $183,000 joint for 2012), you were not eligible to make contributions, and until last year, if your modified adjusted gross income (MAGI) was over $100,000 (single or joint), you could not convert a traditional IRA to a Roth. Outside these contribution limits, most people save for retirement through their employers and most employers do not offer Roth options in their plans. The reason behind this is because Roth accounts are not that well understood and people have been educated to believe that saving on taxes today is the best possible course of action.

TAX-ADVANTAGED MONEY: LIFE INSURANCE
As previously mentioned, the single greatest tax asset that has come from Congress outside of life insurance is the Roth account. Life insurance is the little-known or little-discussed tax asset that holds some of the greatest value in your financial history both during life and upon death. It is by far the best tax-advantaged device available. We traditionally view life insurance as a way to protect our loved ones from financial ruin upon our demise and it should be noted that everyone who cares about someone should

have life insurance. Purchasing a life insurance policy ensures that our loved ones will receive income from the life insurance company to help them pay our final expenses and carry on with their lives without us comfortably when we die. The best part of the life insurance windfall is the fact that nobody will have to pay tax on the money received. This is the single greatest tax-advantaged device available, but it has one downside, we do not get to use it. Only our heirs will.

The little known and discussed part of life insurance is the cash value build-up within whole life and universal life (permanent) policies. Life insurance is not typically seen as an investment vehicle for building wealth and retirement planning, although we should discuss briefly why this thought process should be re-evaluated. Permanent life insurance is generally misconceived as something that is very expensive for a wealth accumulation vehicle because there are mortality charges (fees for the death benefit) that detract from the available returns. Furthermore, those returns do not yield as much as the stock market over the long run. This is why many times you will hear the phrase "buy term and invest the rest," where "term" refers to term insurance.

Let us take a second to review two terms just used in regard to life insurance: term and permanent. Term insurance is an idea with which most people are familiar. You purchase a certain death benefit that will go to your heirs upon death and this policy will be in effect for a certain number of years, typically 10 to 20 years. The 10 to 20 years is the term of the policy and once you have reached that end you no longer have insurance unless you purchase another policy.

Permanent insurance on the other hand has no term involved. It is permanent as long as the premiums continue to be paid. Permanent insurance generally initially has higher premiums than term insurance for the same amount of death benefit coverage and it is this difference that is referred to when people say "invest the rest."

Simply speaking there are significant differences between these two policies that are not often considered when providing a comparative analysis of the numbers. One item that gets lost in the fray when comparing term and permanent insurance is that term usually expires before death. In fact, insurance studies show less than one percent of all term policies pay out death benefit claims. The issue arises when the term expires and the desire to have more insurance is still present.

A term policy with the same benefit will be much more expensive than the original policy and, many times, life events occur, such as cancer or heart conditions, which makes it impossible to acquire another policy and leaves your loved ones unprotected and tax-advantaged legacy planning out of the equation.

Another aspect and probably the most important piece in consideration of the future of taxation is the fact that permanent insurance has a cash accumulation value. Two aspects stand out with the cash accumulation value. First, as the cash accumulation value increases the death benefit will also increase whereas term insurance remains level. Second, this cash accumulation offers value to you during your lifetime rather than to your heirs upon death. The cash accumulation value can be used for tax-advantaged income during your lifetime through policy loans. Most importantly, this tax-advantaged income is available during retirement for distribution planning, all while offering the same typical financial protection to your heirs.

TAX-DEFERRED MONEY

Tax-deferred money is the type of money with which most of people are familiar, but we also briefly reviewed the idea above. Tax-deferred money is typically our traditional IRA, employer sponsored retirement plan or a non-qualified annuity. Essentially, you put money into an investment vehicle that will accumulate in value over time and you do not pay taxes on the earnings that grow these accounts until you distribute them. Once the money is distributed, taxes must be paid. However, the same negative consequences exist with regard to additional taxation and expense in other areas as previously discussed. The cash accumulation value can be used for tax-advantaged income.

TAXABLE MONEY

Taxable money is everything else and is taxable today, later or whenever it is received. These four types of money come down to two distinct classifications: taxable and tax-free. The greatest difference when comparing taxable and tax-advantaged income is a function of how much money we keep after tax. For help in determining what the differences should be, excluding outside factors such as Social Security taxation and AMT, a tax equivalent yield should be used.

TAX-ADVANTAGED IN THE REAL WORLD

To put the tax equivalent yield into perspective, let us look at an example: Bob and Mary are currently retired, living on Social Security and interest from investments and falling within the 25 percent tax bracket. They have a substantial portion of their investments in municipal bonds yielding 6 percent, which is quite comforting in today's market. The tax equivalent yield they would need to earn from a taxable investment would be 8 percent, a 2 percent gap that seems almost impossible given current market volatility. However, something that has never been put into perspective is that the interest from their municipal bonds is subject to taxation on their Social Security benefits (at 21.25 percent). With this, the yield on their municipal bonds would be 4.725 percent, and the taxable equivalent yield falls to 6.3 percent, leaving a gap of only 1.575 percent.

In the end, most people spend their lives accumulating wealth through the best, if not the only vehicle they know, a tax-deferred account. This account is most likely a 401(k) or 403(b) plan offered through our employer and may be supplemented with an IRA that was established at one point or another. As the years go by, people blindly throw money into these accounts in an effort to save for a retirement that we someday hope to reach.

The truth is, most people have an age selected for when they would like to retire, but spend their lives wondering if they will ever be able to actually quit working. To answer this question, you must understand how much money you will have available to contribute toward your needs. In other words, you need to know what your after-tax income will be during this period.

All else being equal, it would not matter if you put your money into a taxable, tax-deferred or tax-advantaged account as long as income tax rates never change and outside factors are never an event. The net amount you receive in the end will be the same.

Unfortunately, this will never be the case. We already know that taxes will increase in the future, meaning we will likely see higher taxes in retirement than during our peak earning years.

Regardless, saving for retirement in any form is a good thing as it appears from all practical perspectives that future government benefits will be cut and taxes will increase. You have the ability to plan today for efficient tax diversification and maximization of our after-tax dollars during your distribution years.

CHAPTER 11 RECAP //

- A closer examination of the debt ceiling and taxes throughout U.S. history points to the benefits of tax diversification.
- Most people are familiar with tax-deferred methods of retirement savings such a traditional IRAs. By taking action now, you can prepare for the rise in taxes by restructuring your assets to include the benefits of free and tax-advantaged money.
- Tax-advantaged money is money you earn without having to pay taxes on. One of the most common forms includes municipal bonds, but be aware these come with many state and federal caveats and complexities.
- Roth IRAs and Life Insurance are two forms of tax-advantaged money that can take advantage of today's lower tax rate when preparing for tomorrow's retirement.

12
HOW WILL YOU BE REMEMBERED?

"Other people have made a difference in my life."

The attitude of many seniors today is that they have spent the majority of their earning years putting their kids through college, helping them buy their first house and so on. They feel as though they have done enough for their kids and their kids are going to be okay, because most of them already have jobs, families and homes of their own.

But then they go and babysit the grandkids. They fall in love with them. They spend an hour or two and say goodbye and then they get a soft spot in their heart for these kids. They think, "I've got to take care of that grandkid in case my son screws up."

While this is said tongue in cheek, many retirees wonder what they can do for their grandkids. They need to take care of their current lifestyle needs and health care costs, yes, but they want to be remembered. Many single retirees and those without grandchildren also want to create a legacy and so they leave behind money to their favorite charity for the same reason: because they want to be remembered.

Today, there is more consideration given to planning a legacy than just maximizing your estate. When most people think about an estate, it may seem like something only the very wealthy have: a stately manor or an enormous business. But a legacy is something else entirely. A legacy is more than the sum total of the financial assets you have accumulated. It is the lasting impression you make on those you leave behind. The dollar and cents are just a small part of a legacy.

A legacy encompasses the stories that others tell about you, shared experiences and values. An estate may pay for college tuition, but a legacy may inform your grandchildren about the importance of higher education and self-reliance.

A legacy may also contain family heirlooms or items of emotional significance. It may be a piece of art your great-grandmother painted, family photos, or a childhood keepsake.

When you go about planning your legacy, certainly explore strategies that can maximize the financial benefit to the ones you care about. But also take the time to ensure that you have organized the whole of your legacy, and let that be a part of the last gift you leave.

Many people avoid planning their legacy until they feel they must. Something may change in your life, like the birth of a grandchild, the diagnosis of a serious health problem, or the death of a close friend or loved one. Waiting for tragedy to strike in order to get your affairs in order is not the best course of action. The emotional stress of that kind of situation can make it hard to make patient, thoughtful decisions. Taking the time to create a premeditated and thoughtful legacy plan will assure that your assets will be transferred where and when you want them when the time comes.

THE BENEFITS OF PLANNING YOUR LEGACY

The distribution of your assets, whether in the form of property, stocks, Individual Retirement Accounts, 401(k)s or liquid assets, can be a complicated undertaking if you haven't left clear instructions about how you want them handled. Not having a plan will cost more money and take more time, leaving your loved ones to wait (sometimes for years) and receive less of your legacy than if you had a clear plan.

Planning your legacy will help your assets be transferred with little delay and little confusion. Instead of leaving decisions about how to distribute your estate to your family, attorneys or financial professionals, preserve your legacy and your wishes by drafting a clear plan at an early age.

And while you know all that, it can still be hard to sit down and do it. It reminds you that life is short, and the relatively complicated nature of sorting through your assets can feel like a daunting task. But one thing is for sure: it is impossible for your assets to be transferred or distributed the way you want at the end of your life if you don't have a plan.

Ask yourself:

- Are my assets up to date?
- Have my primary and contingent beneficiaries been clearly designated?
- Does my plan allow for restriction of a beneficiary?
- Does my legacy plan address minor children that I want to provide with income?
- Does my legacy plan allow for multi-generational payout? Answers to these questions are critical if you want the final

say in how your assets are distributed. In order to achieve your legacy goals, you need a plan.

MAKING A PLAN

Eventually, when your income need is filled and you have sufficient standby money to meet your need for emergencies, travel or other extra expenses you are planning for, whatever isn't used during your lifetime becomes your financial legacy. The money that you do not use during your lifetime will either go to loved ones, unloved ones, charity, or the IRS. The questions is, who would you rather disinherit?

By having a legacy plan that clearly outlines your assets, your beneficiaries and your distribution goals, you can make sure that your money and property is ending up in the hands of the people you determine beforehand. Is it really that big of a deal? It absolutely is. Think about it. Without a clear plan, it is impossible for anyone to know if your beneficiary designations are current and reflect your wishes because you haven't clearly expressed who your beneficiaries are. You may have an idea of who you want your assets to go to, but without a plan, it is anyone's guess. It is also impossible to know if the titling of your assets is accurate unless you have gone through and determined whose name is on the titles. More importantly, if you have not clearly and effectively communicated your desires regarding the planned distribution of your legacy, you and your family may end up losing a large part of it.

As you can see, managing a legacy is more complicated than having an attorney read your will, divide your estate and write checks to your heirs. The additional issue of taxes, Family Maximum Benefit calculations and a host of other decisions rear their heads. Educating yourself about the best options for positioning your legacy assets is a challenging undertaking. Working with a financial professional who is versed in determining the most efficient and effective ways of preserving and distributing your legacy can save you time, money and strife.

So, how do you begin?

Making a Legacy Plan Starts with a Simple List. The first, and one of the largest, steps to setting up an estate plan with a financial professional that reflects your desires is creating a detailed inventory of your assets and debts (if you have any). You need to know what assets you have, who the beneficiaries are, how much they are worth and how they are titled. You can start by identifying and listing your assets. This is a good starting point for working with a financial professional who can then help you determine the detailed information about your assets that will dictate how they are distributed upon your death.

If you are particularly concerned about leaving your kids and grandkids a lifetime of income with minimal taxes, you will want to discuss a Stretch IRA option with your financial professional.

STRETCH IRAS: GETTING THE MOST OUT OF YOUR MONEY

In 1986, the U.S. Congress passed a law that allows for multi-generational distributions of IRA assets. This type of distribution is called a Stretch IRA because it stretches the distribution of the account out over a longer period of time to several beneficiaries. It also allows the account to continue accumulating value throughout your relatives' lifetimes. You can use a Stretch IRA as an income tool that distributes throughout your lifetime, your children's lifetimes and your grandchildren's lifetimes.

Stretch IRAs are an attractive option for those more concerned with creating income for their loved ones than leaving them with a lump sum that may be subject to a high tax rate. With traditional IRA distributions, non-spousal beneficiaries must generally take distributions from their inherited IRAs, whether transferred or not, within five years after the death of the IRA owner. An exception to this rule applies if the beneficiary elects to take distributions over his or her lifetime, which is referred to as stretching the IRA.

Let's begin by looking at the potential of stretching an IRA throughout multiple generations.

> » *In this scenario, Mr. Cleaver has an IRA with a current balance of $350,000. If we assume a five percent annual rate of return, and a 28 percent tax rate, the Stretch IRA turned a $502,625 legacy into more than $1.5 million. Doubling the value of the IRA also provided Mr. Cleaver, his wife, two children and three grandchildren with income. Not choosing the stretch option would have cost nearly $800,000 and had impacts on six of Mr. Cleaver's loved ones.*

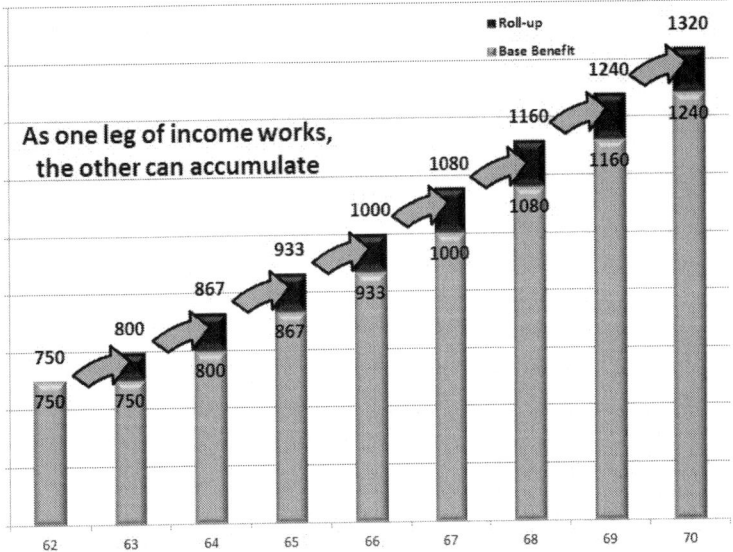

As one leg of income works, the other can accumulate

Unfortunately, many things may also play a role in failing to stretch IRA distributions. It can be tempting for a beneficiary to take a lump sum of money despite the tax consequences. Fortunately, if you want to solidify your plan for distribution, there are options that will allow you to open up an IRA and incorporate "spendthrift" clauses for your beneficiaries. This will ensure your legacy is stretched appropriately and to your specifications. Only certain insurance companies allow this option, and you will not find this benefit with any brokerage accounts. You need to work with a financial professional who has the appropriate relationship with an insurance company that provides this option.

CHAPTER 12 RECAP //

- Your legacy encompasses more than just the physical assets left behind for your children, grandchildren and charities or organizations. It's how you will be remembered.
- Managing a legacy is more complicated than having an attorney read your will, divide your estate, and write checks to your heirs. Issues such as taxes, Family Maximum Benefit calculations and a host of other concerns make it necessary to educate yourself. Working with a financial professional can save you time, money and stress.
- Legacy planning begins with a simple list.

13
LEGACY MISTAKES AND HOW TO AVOID THEM

"What's the worst thing that can happen?"

Thomas organized his assets long ago. He started planning his retirement early and made investment decisions that would meet his needs. With a combination of IRA to Roth IRA conversions, a series of income annuities and a well-planned money management strategy overseen by his financial professional, he easily filled his income gap and was able to focus on ways to accumulate his wealth throughout his retirement. He reorganized his Safe Side and Risk Side Money as he got older. When Thomas retired, he had an income plan created that allowed him to maximize his Social Security benefit. He even had enough to accumulate wealth during his retirement. At this point, Thomas turned his attention to planning his legacy. He wanted to know how he could maximize the amount of money he will pass on to his heirs.

Thomas met with an attorney to draw up a will, but he quickly learned that while having a will was a good plan, it wasn't the most efficient way to distribute his legacy. In fact, relying solely on a will created several roadblocks.

If you're like most people, planning your estate isn't on the top of your list of things to do. Planning your income needs for retirement, managing your assets and just living your life without worrying about how your estate will be handled when you are gone makes legacy planning less than attractive for a Saturday afternoon task. The fact of the matter, however, is that if you don't plan your legacy, someone else will. That someone else is usually a combination of the IRS and other government entities: lawyers, executors, courts, and accountants. Who do you think has the best interests of your beneficiaries in mind?

AVOIDING THE BIG MISTAKES

Unfortunately, even with the best of intentions, mistakes can easily happen when planning for how you will be remembered. In the above story, the two main problems that arose for Thomas were *Probate* and *Unintentional Disinheritance:*

Problem #1: Probate

Probate. Just speaking the word out loud can cause shivers to run down your spine. Probate's ugly reputation is well deserved. It can be a costly, time consuming process that diminishes your estate and can delay the distribution of your estate to your loved ones. Nasty stuff, by any measure. Unless you have made a clear legacy plan and discussed options for avoiding probate, it is highly likely that you have many assets that might pass through probate needlessly. If your will and beneficiary designations aren't correctly structured, some of these assets will go through the probate process, which can turn dollars into cents.

If you have a will, probate is usually just a formality. There is little risk that your will won't be executed per your instructions. The problem arises when the costs and lengthy timeline that probate creates come into play. Probate proceedings are notoriously expensive, lengthy and ponderous. A typical probate process identifies all of your assets and debts, pays any taxes and fees that you owe (including estate tax), pays court fees, and distributes your property and assets to your heirs. This process usually takes at least a year, and can take even longer before your heirs actually receive anything that you have left for them. For this reason, and because of the sometimes exorbitant fees that may be charged by lawyers and accountants during the process, probate has earned a nasty reputation.

Probate can also be a painstakingly public process. Because the probate process happens in court, the assets you own that go through a probate procedure become part of the public record. While this may not seem like a big deal to some, other people don't want that kind of intimate information available to the public.

Additionally, if your estate is entirely distributed via your will, the money that your family may need to cover the costs of your medical bills, funeral expenses and estate taxes will be tied up in probate, which can last up to a year or more. While immediate family members may have the option of requesting immediate cash from your assets during probate to cover immediate health care expenses, taxes, and fees, that process comes with its own set of complications. Choosing alternative methods for distributing your legacy can make life easier for your loved ones and can help them claim more of your estate in a more timely fashion than traditional methods.

A simpler and less tedious approach is to avoid probate altogether by structuring your estate to be distributed outside of the probate process. Two common ways of doing this are by structuring your assets inside a life insurance plan, and by using individual retirement planning tools like IRAs that give you the option of designating a beneficiary upon your death.

Problem #2: Unintentionally Disinheriting Your Family

You would never want to unintentionally disinherit a loved one or loved ones because of confusion surrounding your legacy plan. Unfortunately, it happens. Why? This terrible situation is typically caused by a simple lack of understanding. In particular, mistakes regarding legacy distribution occur with regards to those whom people care for the most: their grandchildren.

One of the most important ways to plan for the inheritance of your grandchildren is by properly structuring the distribution of your legacy. Specifically, you need to know if your legacy is going to be distributed *per stirpes* or *per capita*.

Per Stirpes. *Per stirpes* is a legal term in Latin that means "by the branch." Your estate will be distributed *per stirpes* if you designate each branch of your family to receive an equal share of your estate. In the event that your children predecease you, their share will be distributed evenly between their children — your grandchildren.

Per Capita. *Per capita* distribution is different in that you may designate different amounts of your estate to be distributed to members of the same generation.

Per stirpes distribution of assets will follow the family tree down the line as the predecessor beneficiaries pass away. On the other hand, per capita distribution of assets ends on the branch of the family tree with the death of a designated beneficiary. For example, when your child passes away, in a per capita distribution, your grandchildren would not receive distributions from the assets that you designated to your child.

What the terms mean is not nearly as important as what they do, however. The reality is that improperly titled assets could accidentally leave your grandchildren disinherited upon the death of their parents. It's easy to check, and it's even easier to fix.

A simple way to remember the difference between the two types of distribution goes something like this: "**Stripes are forever and Capita is capped.**"

Another way to avoid complicated legacy distribution problems, and the probate process, is by leveraging a life insurance plan.

LIFE INSURANCE: AN IMPORTANT LEGACY TOOL

One of the most powerful legacy tools you can leverage is a good life insurance policy. Life insurance is a highly efficient legacy tool because it creates money when it is needed or desired the most. Over the years, life insurance has become less expensive, while it offers more features, and it provides longer guarantees.

There are many unique benefits of life insurance that can help your beneficiaries get the most out of your legacy. Some of them include:

- Providing beneficiaries with a tax-free, liquid asset.
- Covering the costs associated with your death.
- Providing income for your dependents.
- Offering an investment opportunity for your beneficiaries.
- Covering expenses such as tuition or mortgage down payments for your children or grandchildren.

Very few people want life insurance, but nearly everyone wants what it does. Life insurance is specifically, and uniquely, capable of creating money when it is needed most. When a loved one passes, no amount of money can remove the pain of loss. And certainly, money doesn't solve the challenges that might arise with losing someone important.

It has been said that when you have money, you have options. When you don't have money, your options are severely limited. You might imagine a life insurance policy can give your family and loved ones options that would otherwise be impossible.

> » *Ben spent the last 20 years building a small business. In so many ways, it is a family business. Each of his three children, Maddie, Ruby and Edward, worked in the shop part-time during high school. But after all three attended college, only Maddie returned to join her father, and eventually will run the business full-time when Ben retires.*
>
> *Ben is able to retire comfortably on Social Security and on-going income from the shop, but the business is nearly his entire financial legacy. It is his wish that Maddie own the business outright, but he also wants to leave an equal legacy to each of his three children.*
>
> *There is no simple way to divide the business into thirds and still leave the business intact for Maddie.*
>
> *Ben ends up buying a life insurance policy to make up the difference. Ruby and Edward will receive their share of an inheritance in cash from the life insurance policy and Maddie will be able to inherit the business intact.*
>
> *Ben is able to accomplish his goals, treat all three children equitably and leave Maddie the business she helped to build.*

If you have a life insurance policy but you haven't looked at it in a while, you may not know how it operates, how much it is worth and how it will be distributed to your beneficiaries. You may also need to update your beneficiaries on your policy. In short, without a comprehensive review of your policy, you don't really know where the money will go or to whom it will go.

If you don't have a life insurance policy but are looking for options to maintain and grow your legacy, speaking with a professional can show you the benefits of life insurance. Many people don't consider buying a life insurance policy until some event in their life triggers it, like the loss of a loved one, an accident or a health condition.

BENEFITS OF LIFE INSURANCE

Life insurance is a useful and secure tool for contingency planning, ensuring that your dependents receive the assets that you want them to have, and for meeting the financial goals you have set for the future. While it bears the name "Life Insurance," it is, in reality, a diverse financial tool that can meet many needs. Today's life insurance policies offer what are known as Living Benefits. These benefits provide the insured additional income while they are still alive should the need arise due to chronic illness or the cost of long term care. Traditionally, the main function of a life insurance policy is to provide financial assets for your survivors. Life insurance is particularly efficient at achieving this goal because it provides a tax-advantaged lump sum of money in the form of a death benefit to your beneficiary or beneficiaries. That financial asset can be used in a number of ways. It can be structured as an investment to provide income for your spouse or children, it can pay down debts, and it can be used to cover estate taxes and other costs associated with death.

Tax liabilities on the estate you leave behind are inevitable. Capital property, for instance, is taxed at its fair market value at the time of your death, unless that property is transferred to your spouse. If the property has appreciated during the time you owned it, taxation on capital gains will occur. Registered Retirement Savings Plans (RRSPs) and other similarly structured assets are also included as taxable income unless transferred to a beneficiary as well. Those are just a few examples of how an estate can become subject to a heavy tax burden. The unique benefits of a life insurance policy provide ways to handle this tax burden, solving any liquidity problems that may arise if your family members want to hold onto an illiquid asset, such as a piece of property or an investment. Life insurance can provide a significant amount of money to a family member or other beneficiary, and that money is likely to remain exempt from taxation or seizure.

One of life insurance's most important benefits is that it is not considered part of the estate of the policy holder. The death benefit that is paid by the insurance company goes exclusively to the beneficiaries listed on the policy. This shields the proceeds of the policy from fees and costs that can reduce an estate, including probate proceedings, attorneys' fees and claims made by creditors. The distribution of your life insurance policy is also unaffected by delays of the estate's distribution, like probate. Your beneficiaries will get the proceeds of the policy in a timely fashion, regardless of how long it takes for the rest of your estate to be settled.

Investing a portion of your assets in a life insurance policy can also protect that portion of your estate from creditors. If you owe money to someone or some entity at the time of your death, a creditor is not able to claim any money from a life insurance policy or an annuity, for that matter. As an exception to this rule, if you had already used the life insurance policy as collateral against a loan. If a large portion of the money you want to dedicate to your legacy is sitting in a savings account, investment or other liquid form, creditors may be able to receive their claim on it before your beneficiaries get anything, that is if there's anything left. A life insurance policy protects your assets from creditors and ensures that your beneficiaries get the money that you intend them to have.

HOW MUCH LIFE INSURANCE DO YOU NEED?

Determining the type of policy and the amount right for you depends on an analysis of your needs. A financial professional can help you complete a needs analysis that will highlight the amount of insurance that you require to meet your goals. This type of personalized review will allow you to determine ways to continue providing income for your spouse or any dependents you may have. A financial professional can also help you calculate the amount of income that your policy should replace to meet the needs of your beneficiaries and the duration of the distribution of that income.

You may also want to use your life insurance policy to meet any expenses associated with your death. These can include funeral costs, fees from probate and legal proceedings, and taxes. You may also want to dedicate a portion of your policy proceeds to help fund tuition or other expenses for your children or grandchildren. You can buy a policy and hope it covers all of those costs, or you can work with a professional who can calculate exactly how much insurance you need and how to structure it to meet your goals. Which would you rather do?

AVOIDING POTENTIAL SNAGS

There are benefits to having life insurance supersede the direction given in a will or other estate plan, but there are also some potential snags that you should address to meet your wishes. For example, if your will instructs that your assets be divided equally between your two children but your life insurance beneficiary is listed as just one of the children, the assets in the life insurance policy will only be distributed to the child listed as the beneficiary. The beneficiary designation of your life insurance supersedes your will's instruction. This is important to understand when designating beneficiaries on a policy you purchase. Work with a professional to make sure that your beneficiaries are accurately listed on your assets, especially your life insurance policies.

USING LIFE INSURANCE TO BUILD YOUR LEGACY

Depending on your goals, there are strategies you can use that could multiply how much you leave behind. Life insurance is one of the most surefire and efficient investment tools for building a substantial legacy that will meet your financial goals.

Here is a brief overview of how life insurance can boost your legacy:

- Life insurance provides an immediate increase in your legacy.
- It provides an income tax-advantaged death benefit for your beneficiaries.
- A good life insurance policy has the opportunity to accumulate value over time.
- It may have an option to include long-term care (LTC) or chronic illness benefits should you require them.

If your Green Money income needs for retirement are met and you have Yellow Money assets that will provide for your future expenses, you may have extra assets that you want to earmark as legacy funds. By electing to invest those assets into a life insurance policy, you can immediately increase the amount of your legacy. Remember, life insurance allows you to transfer a tax-advantaged lump sum of money to your beneficiaries. It remains in your control during your lifetime, can provide for your long-term care needs and bypasses probate costs. And make no mistake, taxes can have a huge impact on your legacy. Not only that, income and assets from your legacy can have tax implications for your beneficiaries, as well.

Here's a brief overview of how taxes could affect your legacy and your beneficiaries:

- The higher your income, the higher the rate at which it is taxed.
- Withdrawals from qualified plans are taxed as income.
- What's more, when you leave a large qualified plan, it ends up being taxed at a high rate.
- If you left a $500,000 IRA to your child, they could end up owing as much as $140,000 in income taxes.
- However, if you could just withdraw $50,000 a year, the tax bill might only be $10,000 per year.

How could you use that annual amount to leave a larger legacy? Luckily, you can leverage a life insurance policy to avoid those tax penalties, preserving a larger amount of your legacy and freeing your beneficiaries from an added tax burden.

> » *When Brenda turned 70 years old, she decided it was time to look into life insurance policy options. She still feels young, but she remembers that her mother died in early 70s, and she wants to plan ahead so she can pass on some of her legacy to her grandchildren just like her grandmother did for her.*
>
> *Brenda doesn't really want to think about life insurance, but she does want the security, reliability and tax-advantaged distribution that it offers. She lives modestly, and her Social Security benefit meets most of her income needs. As the beneficiary of her late husband's Certificate of Deposit (CD), she has $100,000 in an account that she has never used and doesn't anticipate ever needing since her income needs were already met.*
>
> *After looking at several different investment options with a professional, Brenda decides that a Single Premium life insurance policy fits her needs best. She can buy the policy with a $100,000 one-time payment and she is guaranteed that it would provide more than the value of the contract to*

her beneficiaries. If she left the money in the CD, it would be subject to taxes. But for every dollar that she puts into the life insurance policy, her beneficiaries are guaranteed at least that dollar plus a death benefit, and all of it will be tax-free! *For $100,000, Brenda's particular policy offers a $170,000 death benefit distribution to her beneficiaries. By moving the $100,000 from a CD to a life insurance policy, Brenda increases her legacy by 70 percent. Not only that, she has also sheltered it from taxes, so her beneficiaries will be able to receive $1.70 for every $1.00 that she entered into the policy! While buying the policy doesn't allow her to use the money for herself, it does allow her family to benefit from her well-planned legacy.*

MAKE YOUR WISHES KNOWN

Estate taxes used to be a much hotter topic in the mid-2000s when the estate tax limits and exclusions were much smaller and taxed at a higher rate than today. In 2008, estates valued at $2 million or more were taxed at 45 percent. Just two years later, the limit was raised to $5 million dollars taxed at 35 percent. The limit has continued to rise ever since. The limit applies to fewer people than before. Estate organization, however, is just as important as ever, and it affects everyone.

Ask yourself:

- Are your assets actually titled and held the way you think they are?
- Are your beneficiaries set up the way you think they should be?
- Have there been changes to your family or those you desire as beneficiaries?

There is more to your legacy beyond your property, money, investments and other assets that you leave to family members, loved ones and charities. Everyone has a legacy beyond money. You also leave behind personal items of importance, your values and beliefs, your personal and family history, and your wishes. Beyond a will and a plan for your assets, it is important that you make your wishes known to someone for the rest of your personal legacy. When it comes time for your family and loved ones to make decisions after you are gone, knowing your wishes can help them make decisions that honor you and your legacy, and give meaning to what you leave behind. Your professional can help you organize.

Think about your:
- Personal stories / recollections
- Values
- Personal items of emotional significance
- Financial assets
- Do you want to make a plan to pass these things on to your family?

WORKING WITH A PROFESSIONAL

Part of using life insurance to your greatest advantage is selecting the policy and provider that can best meet your goals. Venturing into the jungle of policies, brokers and salespeople can be overwhelming, and can leave you wondering if you've made the best decision. Working with a trusted financial professional can help you cut through the red tape, the "sales-speak" and confusion to find a policy that meets your goals and best serves your desires for your money. If you already have a policy, a financial professional can help you review it and become familiar with the policy's premium, the guarantees the policy affords, its performance, and its features and benefits. A financial professional can also help you make any necessary changes to the policy.

» *When Cheryl turned 88, her daughter finally convinced her to meet with a financial professional to help her organize her assets and get her legacy in order. Although Cheryl is reluctant to let a stranger in on her personal finances, she ends up very glad that she did.*

In the process of listing Cheryl's assets and her beneficiaries, her professional finds a man's name listed as the beneficiary of an old life insurance annuity that she owns. It turns out, the man is Cheryl's ex-husband who is still alive. Had Cheryl passed away before her ex-husband, the annuities and any death benefits that came with them, would have been passed on to her ex-husband. This does not reflect her latest wishes.

Things change, relationships evolve and the way you would like your legacy organized needs to adapt to the changes that happen throughout your life. There may be a new child or grandchild in your family, or you may have been divorced or remarried. A professional will regularly review your legacy assets and ask you questions to make sure that everything is up to date and that the current organization reflects your current wishes.

CHAPTER 13 RECAP //

- You can structure your assets in ways that maximize distributions and decreases taxes to your beneficiaries. Working with a financial professional can help you design a plan that best meets your retirement goals and helps you avoid the ponderous and expensive probate process.

- A financial professional can help review the details of the assets you have designated to be a part of your legacy and make sure that you aren't unintentionally disinheriting your heirs.

- Life insurance provides for the distribution of tax-free, liquid assets to your beneficiaries and can significantly build your legacy. They can also provide Living Benefits to help you pay for the high costs of medical care while you are still living.

- You can take advantage of a "Stretch IRA" to provide income for you, your spouse and your beneficiaries throughout their lifetimes.

- To avoid unintentional disinheritance, understand the difference between the designations *per stirpes* and *per capita*.

14

CHOOSING
A FINANCIAL
PROFESSIONAL

"What does it take to get a happy ending?"

Remember Carol and Dan, the teachers who were waiting to retire? Even though they both had some money in savings, an inheritance and a Social Security benefit to look forward to, they were not looking forward to retirement, They were scared and concerned about outliving their money. They didn't know what kind of tax consequences to expect from their $300,000 inheritance, when to start taking their Social Security benefit, or how to save for the cost of longer term care. Dan's father was in his late 80s and had already depleted his retirement savings due to medical costs. Carol and Dan had a glimpse of *the realities they would be facing down the road, but they didn't know what to do about those concerns.*

Before they met with a financial professional, they had no idea what their retirement would look like.

After doing a financial analysis, they maximized their Social Security benefit by targeting the year and month they would get the most lifetime benefits. They discovered that with both of their retirement pensions and Social Security, they had an income gap of $1,500 a month. Carol wondered if there was a way to structure the inheritance to take care of the shortfall? There was. Using a laddering strategy, they used 70 percent of their funds to purchase three different indexed annuities with lifetime income riders. By putting three different contracts together instead of just one and leaving 20 percent of their money in mutual funds and 10 percent in a money market account, Carol and Dan had income, liquidity and growth. The income riders supported enough guaranteed income for the rest of their life – whether they lived to the average life expectancy age of 84 or if they lived to be 110. Their financial professional also structured their tax situation to fill the gap of the $1,500 with income left over. The money market and mutual funds represent their rainy day/emergency money accounts. Together these tools and strategies will enable Dan and Carol to retire in three years, when they are both 65. Retirement is no longer a looming problem to fear, but a golden opportunity to look forward to.

The above scenario isn't a fairy tale. It's an example of how much you stand to gain by meeting with a financial professional who can help you create a planful approach to your retirement. The concept of Know So and Hope So didn't just apply to their money, it also applied to Dan and Carol. They hoped that they would have enough for retirement and that they had worked hard enough and saved enough to maintain their lifestyle. Working with a financial professional allowed them to know that their income needs were secured and structured to provide them with income for the rest of their lives and with some money to spare.

Now, ask yourself: Is your retirement built on hopes and dreams, or a solid, predictable plan?

IS YOUR FINANCIAL PROFESSIONAL ONE OF THE GOOD GUYS?

It is important to know what you are looking for before trusting a financial professional with the future of your retirement. There are many people that would love to handle your money, but not everyone is qualified to handle it in a way that leads to a holistic approach to creating a solid retirement plan.

The distinction being made here is that you should look for someone that puts your interests first and actively wants to help you meet your goals and objectives. Oftentimes, the products someone sells you matter less than their dedication to making sure that you have a plan that meets your needs.

Professionals take your whole financial position into consideration. They make plans that adjust your risk exposure, invest in tools that secure your desired income during retirement and create investment strategies that allow you to continue accumulating wealth during your retirement for you to use later or to contribute to your legacy. If you buy stocks with a broker, use a different agent for a life insurance policy and have an unmanaged 401(k) through your employer, working with a financial professional will consolidate the management of your assets so you have one trustworthy person quarterbacking all of the team elements of your portfolio. Financial products and investment tools change, but the concepts that lie behind wise retirement planning are lasting. In the end, a financial professional's approach is designed for those serious about planning for retirement. *Can you say the same thing about the person that advises you about your financial life?*

It's easy to see how choosing a financial professional can be one of the most important decisions you can make in your life. Not only do they provide you with advice, they also manage the personal assets that supply your retirement income and contribute to your legacy. So, how do you find a good one?

HOW TO FIND A FINANCIAL PROFESSIONAL YOU CAN TRUST

Taking care to select a financial professional is one of the best things you can do for yourself and for your future. Your professional has influence and control of your investment decisions, making their role in your life more than just important. Your financial security and the quality of your retirement depends on the decisions, investment strategies and asset structuring that you and your professional create.

Working with a professional is different than calling up a broker when you want to buy or trade some stock. This isn't a decision that you can hand off to anyone else. You need to bring your time and attention to the table when it comes to finding someone with whom you can entrust your financial life. Separating the wheat from the chaff will take some work, but you'll be happy you did it.

While no one can tell you exactly who to choose or how to choose them, the following information can help you narrow the field:

- You can start by asking your friends, family and colleagues for referrals. You will want to pay particular attention to the recommendations that you get from others who are in your similar financial situation and who have similar lifestyle choices. The professional for the CEO of your company may have a different skill-set than the skill-set of the professional befitting your cousin who has 3 kids and a Subaru like you. Do follow-up research on the Internet as well. Look up the people who have been recommended to you on websites like LinkedIn that show the work history, referrals and experience of the candidates that you find most attractive. You will also learn about the firms with or for whom they work. The investment philosophies and reputations of the companies they work for will tell you a lot about how they will handle your money.

- The other side of the coin, however, is that everyone and their brother has a recommendation about how you should manage your money and who should manage it for you. From hot stock tips to "the best money manager in the state," people love to share good information that makes them look like they are in-the-know. Nobody wants to talk about the bad stock purchases they made, the times they lost money and the poor selections they made regarding financial professionals or stock brokers. If you decide to take a friend or family member's recommendation, make sure they have a substantial, long-term experience with the financial professional and that their glowing review isn't just based on a one-time "win."

- You can also use online tools like the search function of the Financial Planning Association (http://www.fpanet. org/) and the National Association of Personal Financial professionals (http://www.napfa.org/). Most of the professionals listed on these sites do not earn commissions from selling financial products, but are instead paid on a fee-only basis for their services. It is important to understand how your professional is being paid. It is generally considered preferable to work with a fee-based professional who will not have conflicts of interests between earning a commission and acting in your best interests.

- Many professionals may also be brokers or dealers that can earn commissions on things like life insurance, certain types of annuities and disability insurance. These professionals have most likely intentionally overlapped their roles so that if their clients choose to purchase insurance or investment products that require a broker or dealer, those clients won't have to find an additional person to work with. Again, understanding the role of your professional will help you make your determination.

NARROWING THE FIELD

1. Decide on the Type of Professional with Whom You Want to Work. There are four basic kinds of financial professionals. Many professionals may play overlapping roles. It is important to know a professional's primary function, how they charge for their services and whether they are obligated to act in your best interest.

Registered representatives, better known as stockbrokers or bank / investment representatives, make their living by earning commissions on insurance products and investment services. Stockbrokers basically sell you things. The products from which they make the highest commission are sometimes the products that they recommend to their clients. If you want to make a simple transaction, such as buying or selling a particular stock, a registered representative can help you. Although registered representatives are licensed professionals, if you want to create a structured and planful approach to positioning your assets for retirement, you might want to consider continuing your search.

The term "planner" is often misused. It can refer to credible professionals that are CPAs, CFPs and ChFCs to your uncle's next door neighbor who claims to have a lead on some undervalued stock about to be "discovered." A wide array of people may claim to be planners because there are no requirements to be a planner. The term financial planner, however, refers to someone who is properly registered as an investment advisor and serves as a fiduciary as described below.

Financial professionals are the diamonds in the rough. These Registered Investment Advisors are compensated on a fee basis. They do, however, often have licensure as stockbrokers or insurance agents, allowing them to earn commissions on certain transactions. More importantly, financial professionals are financial fiduciaries, meaning they are required to make financial decisions in your best interest and reflecting your risk tolerance. Investment Advisors are held to high ethical standards and are highly regarded in the financial industry. Financial professionals also often take a more comprehensive approach to asset management. These professionals are trained and credentialed to plan and coordinate their clients' assets in order to meet their goals or retirement and legacy planning. They are not focused on individual stocks, investments or markets. They look at the big picture, the whole enchilada.

Money managers are on par with financial professionals. However, they are often given explicit permission to make investment decisions without advanced approval by their clients.

Understanding who you are working with and what their title is the first step to planning your retirement. While each of the above-mentioned types of financial professionals can help you with aspects of your finances, it is financial professionals who have the most intimate role, the most objective investment strategies and the most unbiased mode of compensation for their services. A financial professional can also help you with the non-financial aspects of your legacy and can help you find ways to create a tax planning strategy to help you save money.

2. Be Objective. At the end of the day, you need to separate the weak from the strong. While you might want a strong personal rapport with your professional, or you may want to choose your professional for their personality and positive attitude, it is more important that you find someone who will give sage advice regarding achieving your retirement goals.

It can be helpful to use a process of elimination to narrow the field of potential professionals. Look into five or six potential leads and cross off your list the ones that don't meet your requirements until only one or two remain. Cross-check your remaining choices against the list of things you need from a professional. Make sure they represent a firm that has the investment tools and products that you desire, and make sure they have experience in retirement planning. That is, after all, the main goal.

Don't be afraid to investigate each of your candidates. You'll want to ask the same questions and look for the same information from everyone you consider so you can then compare them and discern which is best for you. You'll want to take a look at the specific credentials of each professional, their experience and competence, their ethics and fiduciary status, their history and track record, and a list of the services that they offer. The professionals who meet all or most of your qualifications are the ones you will contact for an interview.

Potential professionals should meet your qualifications in the following categories:

- *Credentials:* Look at their experience, the quality of their education, any associations to which they belong and certifications they have earned. Someone who has continued their professional education through ongoing certifications will be more up-to-date on current financial practices compared to someone who got their degree 25 years ago and hasn't done a thing since.

- *Practices:* Look at the track record of your candidates, how they are compensated for their services, the reports and analysis they offer, and their value added services.

- *Services:* Your professional must meet your needs. If you are planning your retirement, you should work with someone who offers services that help you to that end. You want someone who can offer planning, advice on investment strategies, ways to calculate risk, advice on insurance and annuities products, and ways to manage your tax strategy.

- *Ethics:* You want to work with someone who is above board and does things the right way. Vet them by checking their compliance record, current licensing, fiduciary status and, yes, even their criminal record. You never know!

3. Ask for and Check References. Once you have selected two or three professionals that you want to meet, call or email them and ask for references. Every professional should be able to provide you with at least two or three names. In fact, they will probably be eager to share them with you. Most professionals rely on references for validation of their success, quality of services and likability. You should, however, take them with a grain of salt. You have no way to know whether or not references are a professional's friends or colleagues.

It is worth contacting references, however, to check for inconsistencies. Ask each reference the same set of questions to get the same basic information. How long have they been working with the professional? What kind of services have they used and were they happy with them? What type of financial planning did they use the professional for? Were they versed in the type of financial planning that you needed? You can also ask them direct questions to elicit candid responses. What was the full cost of the expenses that your professional charged you? Do the reports and statements you receive come from the same firm? Questions like these can help you get a sense of how well the reference knows their professional and whether or not they are a quality reference.

A good reference is a bit like icing on the cake. It's nice to have them, but nothing speaks louder than a good track record and quality experience. And remember that a good reference, while nice to hear, is relatively cheap. How many times have you heard someone on the golf course or at work telling you how great their stockbroker is? But how many times have you heard about the bad investments or losses they have experienced?

4. Use the Internet. As a final step before picking up the phone and calling your candidates, do some digging to discover if anyone on your list has a history of unlawful or unethical practices, or has been disciplined for any of their professional behavior or decisions. Don't worry, you don't have to hire a private investigator. You can easily find this information on the Financial Industry Regulatory Authority's (FINRA) online BrokerCheck tool: http://www.finra.org/Investors/ToolsCalculators/BrokerCheck/.

You should obviously explore the website of a potential professional and the website of the firm that they represent. The Internet allows you to go beyond the online business card of a professional to gain access to information that they don't control. It may all be good information! Or a brief search of the Internet could reveal a sketchy past. The best part is that the Internet allows you to find helpful information in an anonymous fashion.

Start with Google (www.google.com) and search the name of a potential professional and their firm. Keep your eyes trained on third party sources such as articles, blog posts or news stories that mention the professional. You can also check a professional's compliance records online with the Financial Industry Regulatory Authority (FINRA) and the Securities and Exchange Commission (SEC). If you want to dig deeper, you can combine search terms like "scams," "lawsuits," "suspensions" and "fraud" with a professional's or firm's name to see what information arises. More likely than not, you won't find anything. But if you do, you'll be glad that you checked.

HOW TO INTERVIEW CANDIDATES

After vetting your candidates and narrowing down a list of professionals that you think might be a good fit for you, it's time to start interviewing.

When you meet in person with a professional, you want to take advantage of your time with them. The presentations and information that they share with you will be important to pay attention to, but you will also want to control some aspects of the interview. After a professional has told you what they want you to hear, it's time to ask your own questions to get the specific information you need to make your decision.

Make sure to prepare a list of questions and an informal agenda so that you can keep track of what you want to ask and what points you want the professional to touch on during the interview. Using the same questions and agenda will also allow you to more easily compare the professionals after you have interviewed them all. Remember that these interviews are just that, *interviews*. You are meeting with several professionals to determine with whom you want to work. Don't agree to anything or sign anything during an interview until after you have made your final decision.

It can also be helpful to put a time limit on your interviews and to meet the professionals at their offices. The time limit will keep things on track and will allow structured time for presentations and questions/discussion. By meeting them at their office, you can get a sense of the work environment, the staff culture and attitude, and how the firm does business. If you are unable to travel to a professional's office and must meet them at your home or office, make sure that your interviews are scheduled with plenty of time between so the professionals don't cross each other's paths.

You can use the following questions during an initial interview to get an understanding of how each professional does business and whether they are a good fit for you:

1. How do you charge for your services? How much do you charge? This information should be easy to find on their website, but if you don't see it, ask. Find out if they charge an initial planning fee, if they charge a percentage for assets under their management and if they make money by selling specific financial products or services. If so, you should follow up by asking how much the service costs. This will give you an idea of how they really make their money and if they have incentive to sell certain products over others. Make sure you understand exactly how you will be charged so there are no surprises down the road if you decide to work with this person.

2. What are your credentials, licenses, and certifications? There are Certified Financial Planners (CFPs), Chartered Financial Consultants (ChFCs), Investment Advisor Representatives, Certified Public Accountants (CPAs) and Personal Financial Specialists (PFSs). Whatever their credentials or titles, you want to be sure that the professional you work with is an expert in the field relevant to your circumstances. If you want someone to manage your money, you will most likely look for an Investment Advisor. Someone that works with an independent firm will likely have a team of CPAs, CFPs and other financial experts upon whom they can draw. If you like the professional you are meeting with and you think they might be a good fit, but they don't have the accounting experience you want them to have, ask about their firm and the resources available to them. If they work closely with CPAs that are experienced in your needs, it could be a good match.

3. What are the financial services that you and your firm provide? The question within the question here is, "Can you help me achieve my goals?" Some people can only provide you with investment advice, and others are tax consultants. You will likely want to work with someone that provides a complete suite of financial planning services and products that touch on retirement planning, Social Security maximization, insurance options, legacy and estate structuring, and tax planning. There are also non-financial issues such as health care, long term illness and unexpected family emergencies. A good plan will take into account life situations and factor those in right along with the numbers.

4. What kinds of clients do you work with the most? A lot of financial professionals work within a niche: retirement planning, risk assessment, life insurance, etc. Finding someone who works with other people that are in the same financial boat as you and who have similar goals can be an important way to make sure they understand your needs. While someone might be a crackerjack annuities cowboy, you might not be interested in that option. Ask follow-up questions that will really help you understand where their expertise lies and whether or not their experience lines up with your needs.

5. May I see a sample of one of your financial plans? You wouldn't buy a car without test driving it, and you should not work with a professional without seeing a sample of how they do business. While there is no formal structure that a financial plan has to follow, the variation between professionals can help you find someone who "speaks your language." One professional may provide you with an in-depth analysis that relies heavily on info graphics and diagrams. Someone else may give you a seven page review of your assets and general recommendations. By seeing a sample plan, you can narrow down who presents information in the way that you desire and in ways that you understand.

6. How do you approach investing? You may be entirely in the dark about how to approach your investments, or you might have some guiding principles. Either way, ask each candidate what their philosophy is. Some will resonate with you and some won't. A good professional who has a realistic approach to investing won't promise you the moon or tell you that they can make you a lot of money. Professionals who are successful at retirement planning and full service financial management will tell you that they will listen to your goals, risk tolerance and comfort level with different types of investment strategies. Working with someone that you trust is critical, and this question in particular can help you find out who you can and who you can't.

7. How do you remain in contact with your clients? Does your prospective professional hold annual, quarterly or monthly meetings? How often do *you* want to meet with your professional? Some people want to check in once a year, go over everything and make sure their ducks are all in a row. If any changes over the previous year or additions to their legacy planning strategy came up, they'll do it on that date. Other people want a monthly update to be more involved in the decision making process and to understand what's happening with their portfolio. You basically need to determine the right degree of involvement for both you and your financial professional. You'll also want to feel out how your professional communicates. Do you prefer phone calls or face-to-face meetings? Do you want your professional to explain things to you in detail or to summarize for you what decisions they've made? Is the professional willing to give you their direct phone number or their email address? More importantly, do you want that information and do you want to be able to contact them in those ways?

8. Are you my main contact, or do you work with a team? This is another way of finding out how involved with you your professional will be, and how often they will meet with you. It is also a way to discover how the firm they represent operates and manages their clients. Some professionals will answer their own phone, meet with you regularly and have your home phone number on speed dial. Others will meet with you once a year and have a partner or assistant check in with you every quarter to give you an update. Other companies take an entirely team-based approach whereby clients have a main contact but their portfolio is handled by a team of professionals that represent the firm. One way isn't better than another, but one way will be best for you. Find out how the professional you are interviewing operates before entering into an agreement.

9. How do you provide a unique experience for your clients? This is a polite way of asking, "Why should I work with you?" A professional should have a compelling answer to this question that connects with you. Their answer will likely touch on their investment philosophy, their communication style and their expertise. If you hear them describing strengths and philosophies that resonate with you, keep them on your list. Some professionals will tell you that they will make investments with your money that match your values, others will say they will maximize your returns and others will say they will protect your capital while structuring your assets for income. Whatever you're looking for in a professional, you will most likely find it in the answer to this question.

This last question you will want to ask *yourself* after you've met with someone who you are considering hiring:

10. Did they ask questions and show signs that they were interested in working with me? A professional who will structure your assets to reflect your risk tolerance and to position you for a comfortable retirement must be a good listener. You will want to pass by a professional who talks non-stop and tells you what to do without listening to what you want them to do. If you felt they listened well and understood your needs, and seemed interested and experienced in your situation, then they might be right for you.

THE IMPORTANCE OF INDEPENDENCE

Not all investment firms and financial professionals are created equal. The information in this book has systematically shown that leveraging investments for income and accumulation in today's market requires new ideas and modern planning. In short, you need innovative ideas to come up with the creative solutions that will provide you with the retirement that you want. Innovation thrives on independence. No matter how good a financial professional is, the firm that they represent needs to operate on principles that make sense in today's economy. Remember, advice about money has been around forever. Good advice, however, changes with the times.

Timing the market, relying on the sale of stocks for income and banking on high treasury and bond returns are not strategies. They aren't even realistic ways to make money or to generate income. Working with an independent agent can help you break free from the old ways of thinking and position you to create a realistic retirement plan.

Working with an independent professional who relies on fee-based income tied to the success of their performance will also give you greater peace of mind. When you do well, they do well, and that's the way it should be. Your independent financial professional will make sure that:

- Your assets are organized and structured to reflect your risk tolerance.
- Your assets will be available to you when you need them and in the way that you need them.

- You will have a lifetime income that will support your lifestyle through your retirement.
- You are handling your taxes as efficiently as possible.
- Your legacy is in order.
- Your Red Money is turned into Yellow Money, and is managed in your best interest.

IT'S WORTH IT!

Finding, interviewing and selecting a financial professional can seem like a daunting task. And honestly, it will take a good amount of work to narrow the field and find the one you want. In the end, it is worth the blood, sweat and tears. Your retirement, lifestyle, assets and legacy are on the line. The choices you make today will have lasting impacts on your life and the life of your loved ones. Working with someone you trust and know you can rely on to make decisions that will benefit you is invaluable. The work it takes to find them is something you will never regret.

Here is a recap of why working with a financial professional is the best retirement decision you can make:

CHAPTER 14 RECAP //

- A good financial professional puts your needs and happiness first. Your risk tolerance, goals, objectives, needs, wants, liquidity concerns and timeline worries should be the focus of the meeting before they try to sell you any products. A good plan must also be revisited to make sure it is still a good fit for your current life situation.
- Understand the source of the financial advice you are given. There are only three legal ways to obtain financial advice: insurance only agents, registered representatives – also known as brokers – and Registered Investment Advisors (RIAs). To avoid confusion, educate yourself about the difference between suitability and fiduciary standards, how these

professionals are compensated and what they are qualified to do for you.

- To find a professional you can trust, start by asking family and friends for referrals. Make sure to do your due diligence and check out the references of anyone who is recommended to you. Look for resources online such as the Financial Planning Association and the National Association of Personal Financial professionals.

- When interviewing candidates, make sure you understand how they charge for their services. Also look for credentials, licenses and certifications. Ask questions such as: How often do you check in with your clients? Do you offer a Social Security Optimization report? May I see a sample of one of your financial plans? And how do you approach investing? These questions will help ensure that you and your professional are a good fit for each other.

GLOSSARY

ANNUAL RESET *(ANNUAL RATCHET, CLIQUET)* – Crediting methods measuring index movement over a one year period. Positive interest is calculated and credited at the end of each contract year and cannot be lost if the index subsequently declines. Say that the index increased from 100 to 110 in one year and the indexed annuity had an 80 percent participation rate. The insurance company would take the 10 percent gross index gain for the year (110-100/100), apply the participation rate (10 percent index gain x 80 percent rate) and credit 8 percent interest to the annuity. But, what if in the following year the index declined back to 100? The individual would keep the 8 percent interest earned and simply receive zero interest for the down year. An annual reset structure preserves credited gains and treats negative index periods as years with zero growth.

ANNUITANT – The person, usually the annuity owner, whose life expectancy is used to calculate the income payment amount on the annuity.

ANNUITY – An annuity is a contract issued by an insurance company that often serves as a type of savings plan used by individuals looking for long term growth and protection of assets that will likely be needed within retirement.

AVERAGING – Index values may either be measured from a start point to an end point (point-to-point) or values between the start point and end point may be averaged to determine an ending value. Index values may be averaged over the days, weeks, months or quarters of the period.

BENEFICIARY – A beneficiary is the person designated to receive payments due upon the death of the annuity owner or the annuitant themselves.

BONUS RATE – A bonus rate is the "extra" or "additional" interest paid during the first year (the initial guarantee period), typically used as an added incentive to get consumers to select their annuity policy over another.

CALL OPTION *(ALSO SEE PUT OPTION)* – Gives the holder the right to buy an underlying security or index at a specified price on or before a given date.

CAP – The maximum interest rate that will be credited to the annuity for the year or period. The cap usually refers to the maximum interest credited after applying the participation rate or yield spread. If the index methodology showed a 20 percent increase, the participation rate was 60 percent and the maximum interest cap was 10 percent, the contract would credit 10 percent interest. A few annuities use a maximum gain cap instead of a maximum interest cap with the participation rate or yield spread applied to the lesser of the gain or the cap. If the index methodology showed a 20 percent increase, the participation rate was 60 percent and the maximum gain cap was 10 percent, the contract would credit 6 percent interest.

COMPOUND INTEREST – Interest is earned on both the original principal and on previously earned interest. It is more favorable than simple interest. Suppose that your original principal was $1 and your interest rate was 10 percent for five years. With simple interest, your value is ($1 + $0.10 interest each year) = $1.50. With compound interest, your value is ($1 x 1.10 x 1.10 x 1.10 x 1.10 x 1.10) = $1.61. The advantage of compound interest over simple interest becomes greater as each subsequent period passes.

CREDITING METHOD *(ALSO SEE METHODOLOGY)* – The formula(s) used to determine the excess interest that is credited above the minimum interest guarantee.

DEATH BENEFITS – The payment the annuity owner's estate or beneficiaries will receive if he or she dies before the annuity matures. On most annuities, this is equal to the current account value. Some annuities offer an enhanced value at death via an optional rider that has a monthly or annual fee associated with it.

EXCESS INTEREST – Interest credited to the annuity contract above the minimum guaranteed interest rate. In an indexed annuity the excess interest is determined by applying a stated crediting method to a specific index or indices.

FIXED ANNUITY – A contract issued by an insurance company guaranteeing a minimum interest rate with the crediting of excess interest determined by the performance of the insurer's general account. Index annuities are fixed annuities.

FIXED DEFERRED ANNUITY – With fixed annuities, an insurance company offers a guaranteed interest rate plus safety of your principal and earnings ((subject to the claims-paying ability of the insurance company). Your interest rate will be reset periodically, based on economic and other factors, but is guaranteed to never fall below a certain rate.

FREE WITHDRAWALS – Withdrawals that are free of surrender charges.

INDEX – The underlying external benchmark upon which the crediting of excess interest is based, also a measure of the prices of a group of securities.

IRA *(INDIVIDUAL RETIREMENT ACCOUNT)* – An IRA is a tax-advantaged personal savings plan that lets an individual set aside money for retirement. All or part of the participant's contributions may be tax deductible, depending on the type of IRA chosen and the participant's personal financial circumstances. Distributions from many employer-sponsored retirement plans may be eligible to be rolled into an IRA to continue tax-deferred growth until the funds are needed. An annuity can be used as an IRA; that is, IRA funds can be used to purchase an annuity.

IRA ROLLOVER – IRA rollover is the phrase used when an individual who has a balance in an employer-sponsored retirement plan transfers that balance into an IRA. Such an exchange, when properly handled, is a tax-advantaged transaction.

LIQUIDITY – The ease with which an asset is convertible to cash. An asset with high liquidity provides flexibility, in that the owner can easily convert it to cash at any time, but it also tends to decrease profitability.

MARKET RISK – The risk of the market value of an asset fluctuating up or down over time. In a fixed or fixed indexed annuity, the original principal and credited interest are not subject to market risk. Even if the index declines, the annuity owner would receive no less than their original principal back if they decided to cash in the policy at the end of the surrender period. Unlike a security, indexed annuities guarantee the original premium and the premium is backed by, and is as safe as, the insurance company that issued it (subject to the claims-paying ability of the insurance company).

METHODOLOGY *(ALSO SEE CREDITING METHOD)* – The way that interest crediting is calculated. On fixed indexed annuities, there are a variety of different methods used to determine how index movement becomes interest credited.

MINIMUM GUARANTEED RETURN *(MINIMUM INTEREST RATE)* – Fixed indexed annuities typically provide a minimum guaranteed return over the life of the contract. At the time that the owner chooses to terminate the contract, the cash surrender value is compared to a second value calculated using the minimum guaranteed return and the higher of the two values is paid to the annuity owner.

OPTION – A contract which conveys to its holder the right, but not the obligation, to buy or sell something at a specified price on or before a given date. After this given date the option ceases to exist. Insurers typically buy options to provide for the excess interest potential. Options may be American style whereby they may be exercised at any time prior to the given date, or they may have to be exercised only during a specified window. Options that may only be exercised during a specified period are European-style options.

OPTION RISK – Most insurers create the potential for excess interest in an indexed annuity by buying options. Say that you could buy a share of stock for $50. If you bought the stock and it rose to $60 you could sell it and net a $10 profit. But, if the stock price fell to $40 you'd have a $10 loss. Instead of buying the actual stock, we could buy an option that gave us the right to buy the stock for $50 at any time over the next year. The cost of the option is $2. If the stock price rose to $60 we would exercise our option, buy the stock at $50 and make $10 (less the $2 cost of the option). If the price of the stock fell to $40, $30 or $10, we wouldn't use the option and it would expire. The loss is limited to $2 – the cost of the option.

PARTICIPATION RATE – The percentage of positive index movement credited to the annuity. If the index methodology determined that the index increased 10 percent and the indexed annuity participated in 60 percent of the increase, it would be said that the contract has a 60 percent participation rate. Participation rates may also be expressed as asset fees or yield spreads.

POINT-TO-POINT – A crediting method measuring index movement from an absolute initial point to the absolute end point for a period. An index had a period starting value of 100 and a period ending value of 120. A point-to-point method would record a positive index movement of 20 [120-100] or a 20 percent positive movement [(120-100)/100]. Point-to-point usually refers to annual periods; however the phrase is also used instead of term end point to refer to multiple year periods.

PREMIUM BONUS – A premium bonus is additional money that is credited to the accumulation account of an annuity policy under certain conditions.

PUT OPTION *(ALSO SEE CALL OPTION)* – Gives the holder the right to sell an underlying security or index at a specified price on or before a given date.

QUALIFIED ANNUITIES *(QUALIFIED MONEY)* – Qualified annuities are annuities purchased for funding an IRA, 403(b) tax-deferred annuity or other type of retirement arrangements. An IRA or qualified retirement plan provides the tax deferral. An annuity contract should be used to fund an IRA or qualified retirement plan to benefit from an annuity's features other than tax deferral, including the safety features, lifetime income payout option and death benefit protection.

REQUIRED MINIMUM DISTRIBUTION *(RMD)* – The amount of money that Traditional, SEP and SIMPLE IRA owners and qualified plan participants must begin distributing from their retirement accounts by April 1 following the year they reach age 70.5. RMD amounts must then be distributed each subsequent year.

RETURN FLOOR – Another way of saying minimum guaranteed return.

ROTH IRA – Like other IRA accounts, the Roth IRA is simply a holding account that manages your stocks, bonds, annuities, mutual funds and CD's. However, future withdrawals (including earnings and interest) are typically tax-advantaged once the account has been open for five years and the account holder is age 59.5.

RULE OF 72 – Tells you approximately how many years it takes a sum to double at a given rate. It's handy to be able to figure out, without using a calculator, that when you're earning a 6 percent return, for example, by dividing 6 percent into 72, you'll find that it takes 12 years for money to double. Conversely, if you know it took a sum twelve years to double you could divide 12 into 72 to determine the annual return (6 percent).

SIMPLE INTEREST *(ALSO SEE COMPOUND INTEREST)* – Interest is only earned on the principal balance.

SPLIT ANNUITY – A split annuity is the term given to an effective strategy that utilizes two or more different annuity products – one designed to generate monthly income and the other to restore the original starting principal over a set period of time.

STANDARD & POOR'S 500 *(S&P 500)* – The most widely used external index by fixed indexed annuities. Its objective is to be a benchmark to measure and report overall U.S. stock market performance. It includes a representative sample of 500 common stocks from companies trading on the New York Stock Exchange, American Stock Exchange, and NASDAQ National Market System. The index represents the price or market value of the underlying stocks and does not include the value of reinvested dividends of the underlying stocks.

STOCK MARKET INDEX – A report created from a type of statistical measurement that shows up or down changes in a specific financial market, usually expressed as points and as a percentage, in a number of related markets, or in an economy as a whole (i.e. S&P 500 or New York Stock Exchange).

SURRENDER CHARGE – A charge imposed for withdrawing funds or terminating an annuity contract prematurely. There is no industry standard for surrender charges, that is, each annuity product has its own unique surrender charge schedule. The charge is usually expressed as a percentage of the amount withdrawn prematurely from the contract. The percentage tends to decline over time, ultimately becoming zero.

TRADITIONAL IRA – See <u>IRA (Individual Retirement Account)</u>

TERM END POINT – Crediting methods measuring index movements over a greater timeframe than a year or two. The opposite of an annual reset method. Also referred to as a term point-to-point method. Say that the index value was at 100 on the first day of the period. If the calculated index value was at 150 at the end of the period the positive index movement would be 50 percent (150-100/100). The company would credit a percentage of this movement as excess interest. Index movement is calculated and interest credited at the end of the term and interim movements during the period are ignored.

TERM HIGH POINT *(HIGH WATER MARK)* – A type of term end point structure that uses the highest anniversary index level as the end point. Say that the index value was at 100 on the first day of the period, reached a value of 160 at the end of a contract year during the period, and ended the period at 150. A term high point method would use the 160 value – the highest contract anniversary point reached during the period, as the end point and the gross index gain would be 60 percent (160-100/100). The company would then apply a participation rate to the gain.

TERM YIELD SPREAD – A type of term end point structure which calculates the total index gain for a period, computes the annual compound rate of return deducts a yield spread from the annual rate of return and then recalculates the total index gain for the period based on the net annual rate. Say that an index increased from 100 to 200 by the end of a nine year period. This is the equivalent of an 8 percent compound annual interest rate. If the annuity had a 2 percent term yield spread this would be deducted from the annual interest rate (8 percent-2 percent) and the net rate would be credited to the contract (6 percent) for each of the nine years. Total index gain may also be computed by using the highest anniversary index level as the end point.

VARIABLE ANNUITY – A contract issued by an insurance company offering separate accounts invested in a wide variety of stocks and/or bonds. The investment risk is borne by the annuity owner. Variable annuities are considered securities and require appropriate securities registration.

1035 EXCHANGE – The 1035 exchange refers to the section of tax code that allows annuity owners the flexibility to exchange one annuity for another without incurring any immediate tax liabilities. This action is most often utilized when an annuity holder decides they want to upgrade an annuity to a more favorable one, but they do not want to activate unnecessary tax liabilities that would typically be encountered when surrendering an existing annuity contract.

401(K) ROLLOVER – See IRA Rollover

Made in the USA
Lexington, KY
26 January 2015